A FEAR OF BECOMING A MAN

Richard D. Sutton

Copyright Page

A Fear of Becoming a Man
Copyright © October 24, 2016

Dedication Page

This is dedicated to all the believers and go-getters that know the word can't, is not a word that lives in our vocabulary.

Table of Contents

Dwight George Jones,
The Original Mr. PDQ

Josephine Sutton

Three Generations

Foreword

I began reading Fear of Becoming a Man by Mr. Richard Sutton for two reasons, one to support the work and passion of one of my fellow Shaw University classmates and second, to hear his perspective on black manhood. As an elementary school administrator, with over 15 years of teaching and over five years of administration experience, I found the narrative on black youth have not changed much. Black males are still underperforming academically, and they are the highest subgroup of children suspended or expelled from school.

Mr. Sutton's, Fear of Becoming a Man, is relevant and a poignant account of his personal experiences that translates a shared experience of our black and brown boys within the public- school system. With each page, I found his book revealing and filled with passion for the generation of young men and boys who have yet become old enough to understand the significance of the choices they are making on their future lives.

Strikingly noteworthy, he takes his readers through his journey, providing an insightful examination of how black and brown boys could be sitting in classrooms overlooked by teachers and school administrators because they have no behavior issues and yet they remain unmotivated, and unengaged learners. This is what broke my heart. Mr. Sutton reminds his readers that there isn't a one-size fit all for the black and brown boys within any school system. Instead of casting blame and criticism, Mr. Sutton encourages his readers to become more aware of the pastoral care and instructional concern we give to our young men through a supportive stance rather than a fix-it, exit strategy.

Mr. Sutton's book gives women, a glimpse into the heart of black manhood that is often deeply hidden by the misconceptions, and mischaracterizations Black men have faced in the ever-changing society. From family, to media, and the overall social expectations, Black women have been influenced by what we have been told about our men, and what we have experienced. Looking at black manhood through the lens of Mr. Sutton's account, allow women to walk away wanting to know more about the black men we love.

Mr. Sutton's casual conversational style of writing allows his readers to walk through years of heart-felt experiences, from the ups and downs of his childhood to the challenges of young adulthood that inspires compassion for the young black men in our communities.

~Dr. Renette S. Coleman

Introduction

Traits of my truth in as honest form as I know. In my journey towards manhood and its transparent challenges, I was unprepared to walk this path of failure, self-doubt and strong insecurities the challenges of becoming a strong black man. My journey to find out who I was, as well as who I would become to tell this story, of a kid from the urban jungles of Philadelphia, Pa.

Mozell Sutton, my angel

CHAPTER ONE: ODDS YOU WON'T MAKE IT

What do you do when the odds are stacked up against you? There are many stories of different people and their rough life coming up in the hood. My life wasn't as rough as some, but there were some hard times. Growing up as a young black male was tough enough, but there were other challenges that significantly impacted my life.

Tuesday July 13, 1976 was a cool 72 degrees. It was my turn to enter the world! My mother was a scared 21-year-old, about to have her first child. So many worries and questions she had. Whelp, on that cool day in July, there was no turning back. *Let me out, it's my turn to enter the world*! I guess I was trying too hard to make my exit because my mother (my queen) stopped breathing. The oxygen had been cut off from me. The doctors had to act quickly and made an incision in her throat to get air circulating to me. There was no time; I was actually coming into the world lifeless for almost five minutes. Years later, as I heard the story being told, I thought to myself, *what an entrance*! My mother and I have a bond like no other, plus matching scars for life. She wears hers on her throat, and I wear mine on my right wrist. I came into this world as a fighter. Who knew it was preparation for my life journey, this little black boy from the Germantown section of Philly.

As a child, I can remember it being my mother and I, in my younger years and she had to be the most overprotective mother in history. I remember being in church every Sunday listening to my mother sing. She sounded like an angel on Earth, I swear to you. I always thought my mother should have been a professional songstress, as I recall always watching people in the church come to tears every time she would sing. My mother loved me hard, and she acted as only a single parent with their first child would, or at least that was my experience. I remember back when I was about four or five years old, traveling to Tallahassee, Florida to visit Dwight George Jones who just happened to be my father. He was serving time in a federal prison. My mother, grandmother and older sister, who's my father's older daughter from a previous relationship, on Amtrak running wild having fun on our journey to see our father.

This would be an interesting trip that would become planted in my conscious mind to this very day. This trip was cool because we had taken Amtrak from 30th Street Station here in Philadelphia, to Florida, and I remember running up and down that train with my sister having the time of my life. Once we arrived in Florida, it was straight to the hotel, we unpacked and were on to fun. The funny thing is, I don't recall knowing our purpose in going to Florida until we arrived and saw my father the next day, which was such an awesome feeling. I remember running up to him and jumping into his arms hugging him as tight as possible.

To this day, I don't remember seeing any police or handcuffs when we saw him, so in my young mind I don't even think I was aware he was in prison. A few days in of enjoying the trip to the Sunshine State, I almost died. Yeah, this death theme is defined by, never give up and don't count me out.

My big sister, whom I've always admired even to this day, was like my super-shero, anything she did I would attempt it and this was clear on a hot sunny Florida afternoon. My Mother and grandmother let my sister, who's six years older, and myself go out to the hotel pool. My sister was like a fish in water when it came to swimming, but I had never been in a pool prior to this trip. I'm not sure what I was thinking when I decided to follow her as she jumped into the pool of five feet of water and swim down to the deeper end of 12 feet. Unbeknownst to my sister, I decided to follow her and jump in behind her; now remember I've never had a swim lesson in my life, nor had I ever been in a pool prior to arriving in Florida. Oh! Why did I do that? I jumped in and immediately started to drown. To this day, I remember looking at the people watching me as I was drowning, a four-year-old kid being watched by adults as my life was slipping away from me in five feet of water.

There was nothing but white people standing around me watching me drown. It had to have been one of the scariest events in my life, because I thought I was truly about to die, and my sister didn't even know I had jumped in the water behind her so she wouldn't know to come help me. But clearly, it wasn't my time, because the next thing I know a hand grabbed me by my arm pulled me up out of that water. It was my mother with her eyes as wide as a fifty-cent piece. After making sure I was ok, I swear she beat my butt for the next hour for jumping into that pool. The next day my father was back, out on furlough to visit us at the hotel. He jumped in the pool after hearing what happened and wanted to teach me how to swim, but after my experience and the ass whipping my mother had given me, I wanted no parts of that pool. Looking back now, most would say that I was traumatized by the experience of the previous day. You know I never touched another pool until sixth grade. The fear of water has dissipated, and now I have this thing for water; it soothes my mind and soul. I learned how to swim but never learned how to tread water, and because of that some say I still don't truly know how to swim. I mentioned fear, because I feel a lot of times we allow fear to reroute our potential in life; coming from the inner city you could assume we would have "no fear", but that's far from the truth. Growing up, I had the biggest admiration, like most little boys, for their father. My father was a very smooth, super intelligent, street dude who had a reputation for standing up for the little guy or the individuals who were unable to stand up for themselves. Yes, my father ran the streets, sold drugs and did some gang-warring. They nicknamed him PDQ, which stood for Pretty Damn

Quick because he was a really good fighter and also had strong morals. If that makes any sense to you at all, this goes to show that when you come from a good upbringing, no matter how much you stray away from your base, those moral standards and faith-based principles will hold their ground. I never had the opportunity to meet my grandfather due to him passing away before I was born, but my grandmother was a very sharp, strong little old lady who played no games. My father was raised with five siblings; four brothers and one sister.

My grandmother Sarah Jones was a very spiritual, faith-based woman who worked a lot but always made sure she found time to make it to church every Sunday. I believe even though my father was into what he was into, I think he never wanted to disappoint my grandmother, or at least he attempted not to as much as possible. As a child, I would love to hang out with him, as he would call me by my nickname that he gave me, "Daddy Rich" and make me wear my hat ace deuce, which meant slightly to the side. Oh! How I loved every opportunity to spend time with my father. He would take me with him to see his parole officer, and to hang out with him at his friend's house or the bar, where I would sit around and listen to old school R&B while he played cards and laughed with friends. To this day, because of hanging out with my father I have such a connection to old school R&B, yeah, I know you're like who doesn't, but my connection is a little different almost as if I grew up in the 60's or 70's because of how my father and his friends would jam to old school music. When I look back over my life, I only remember seeing my mother and father in each other's presence maybe twice, and with that being said my mother had a sort of admiration for my father who I think was her first love. My mother always says that she can remember what my father had on from head to toe when she first met him. To be honest I've always been astonished by this. Why you ask? Because think about it: how impressive one has to have been for someone to remember exactly what one had on over 30-plus years later? I truly loved my father, but his absence during my early teens to adult years, had a true impact on me walking into manhood. I never had the opportunity to really know my father as a man one-on-one, and all my memories of him are from my very early childhood years.

My father was around, just not always present. I remember one time coming home from school; this was back in my ninth-grade year of high school. At this time, I had just moved to the

West Oak Lane section of the city with my aunt and

her family, summer of 1989. My grandmother,

Sarah Jones, had just relocated from the

Germantown area of the city, where she and my

father and three brothers had lived the majority of

my life, to West Oak Lane as well. I started high

school in this new area of the city and started to

have some issues with a few of the dudes from the

area. This trouble snowed-balled into me fighting

almost every day for an entire week. Well, this one

day I had just gotten off the bus coming home from

school and ran into a group of the dudes that I had

been fighting all week. I was scared thinking they

were about to jump me, I didn't want to show any

fear so I stood there ready to fight but didn't feel

safe and took off running up the block to see if my

father was home. I rang the doorbell and who came

to the door, my father. I guess he could see the

stress and the fear in my face so he asked me what was wrong? Here is one of those times indirectly my father showed me why I should always stand up for myself. I told my father what was going on and he said to me, *"sit down while I throw on some clothes, we are going back down there."* I'm looking like what? He said, *"you never allow anyone to build fear in your heart with coward moves* so *we are going back down there."* My father gets dressed and out the door we go. As we walked back down the hill to find these dudes I remember my father not saying a word but being focused in the moment. We find the group of kids; as I stand there my father says, *"which one of you wants to fight my son?"*

Now they're a little caught off guard so my father says, *"look, what's not going to happen is any of you jumping my son, but what he will do is fight each one of you as I stand here and make sure he's safe."* That day showed me that I had to always be willing to take a stand because running isn't always the best option. My father had his way of doing things even though we never had that father-son talk about becoming a man. His ability to be around at times and to be missing at other times was one that always perplexed me, once I was old enough to realize he was absent more than he was present as a father. One of the things I always respected about my mother, is no matter what, she never spoke negatively of my father, even though he wasn't always doing what he should have been doing as a father.

CHAPTER TWO: DO NOT RESUSCITATE

On my 29th birthday, I received an early A.M. call from my older sister telling me we needed to go to the hospital.

Go to the hospital for what?

Dad was in the hospital and it didn't look good.

My heart dropped, I jumped up to get dressed with my heart racing. I thought to myself, *damn dad why now?* My mind was running crazy, like damn, my father may be dying and I couldn't remember the last time I physically saw or spoke with my father prior to that day. It had to have been one of the hardest days of my adult life, I swear. I showed up at the hospital/jail. Yeah, I said jail; my father was locked up so he was in a prison hospital.

My two sisters and I sat with my father as he sat slumped over in a wheelchair not saying a word to us. I remember my younger sister saying, *'Dad you know today is Richard's birthday.'* He said not a word as he continued to sit slumped over as his three kids made the attempt to spark a conversation with him. As the nurse informed us that our time was up and she rolled my father out of the room, he stopped the nurse, raised his head and said: "Deanna, make sure you sign the do not resuscitate form." Those were the last words I ever heard from my father; on July 17, 2005, he passed away.

With the passing of my father, it was one of the hardest deaths I ever had to deal with. He and I were not the closest, and prior to his death I hadn't seen or spoken to my father in years, but he was the world to me. It had taken a toll on my personal and professional life. His passing was very hard for me

because I felt like I never had the opportunity to talk
with my father as an adult, nor did I get to ask him
questions about life and becoming a man. I never
had the opportunity to ask him why he wasn't there
for me through my teen and early adult years; or
why he never sat me down to discuss what it took to
become a strong black man in these United States.
My struggles with the loss of my father took me
about four years after his death to truly get over.
But honestly, I think you never truly get over the
loss of a parent, especially when you feel like you
were abandoned, so you always have this sense of
emptiness. For example, I hadn't heard a lot about
how smart my father was and I didn't find out that
he had attended North Carolina A&T University
until after his death. That's very significant to me
because I ended up attending an HBCU as well, but
would have attended NC A&T because he did. I

ended up attending college by sheer coincidence and the need to get out on my own. I wanted to get out of my aunt's house and Philadelphia, after high school, and going to college was a sure way out. You may be thinking, well if he had access to his father why didn't he just go talk with him? To be brutally honest, it was pride and anger that I allowed to cloud my judgment to approach my father. It has to be one of my biggest life regrets. My father has a very strong presence about him, which demanded respect, so I truly believe in some ways it intimidated me without me recognizing it.

Truth is, I feel had I gone to him he would have had an honest and open conversation with me, but I do feel like my father as strong as he was, had some strong internal struggles of his own which stagnated his true potential. I believe I'm so much like him in so many ways. Had I had taken the opportunity to talk to him as a man, many of my struggles that I have had over the years, wouldn't have been as much of a struggle because I would have had some guidance to refer to. My father's absence became more relevant my pre-teen years and on. It wasn't that he wasn't around, he just was not present, but as I have stated he was always somewhere that he could be found. Through family or friends, my siblings and I could find him but our anger kept us from making the effort to reach out. It was that *he's the father I'm the child mentality.*

See there was a level of emptiness that I struggled with as a child because not having my mother and father around and active in my life was hard for me. Even though my Aunt Rochelle never made me feel like she didn't love me, there was this sense *of I'm not her child, I'm her nephew* that always laid in the back of my thoughts. The apparent absence of both my parents has always had a strong hold on me, but the one thing I can say about my father is he never missed the graduation of any of my three other siblings or myself. I've tried to bury it in the back of my mind but emptiness isn't something you can just hide away like luggage. Here I am trying to figure out this manhood thing, and actually have no one to really explain what it means or what it's supposed to look like. I had this perception of what it means but it's just that, a perception; I truly believe that as a young male with nine uncles in total between my father's four brothers and my mother's five brothers, becoming a man should have been a no-brainer. I've learned that being a man is so much deeper than that of the surface falsehoods that are perpetuated by society on a daily basis. Not having any instructions or true role models, it makes the struggle even more difficult than it needs to be. With the struggles of not having my father, I also witnessed the devastating impact drugs had on my family. I know drugs played a key part in the dismantling of the men in my family, but I still feel it's all a choice they all decided to make. The thing I find crazy about my uncles, was that most of them had a trade that they were very proficient in like plumbing, electrician, brick masonry, and painting. Not one of them ever, to my knowledge, took any of us under their wing to teach any of their nephews these skills to have a trade under our belt. I do believe this wasn't a priority because they didn't see it through the same lens, which I now see. Also, I'm not fully aware of their struggles as black men, but they all had a sense of strength about them; which I feel myself and my other male cousin inherited.

These are vital survival skills that could have benefited us in life as men, which would have given us strong tangible skills that could have been utilized in an entrepreneurial aspect or as a career path with a company. I say all this to say, the journey to becoming a man has so many twists and turns and with no clear understanding of what being a man is, makes it even more complex.

CHAPTER THREE: THICK
AS THIEVES

In my younger years, mother and I were thick as thieves, until around the age of ten when she met the now father of my three younger siblings. See growing up my mother had a few suitors, and "yes" I have a very beautiful mother, who again has the voice of an angel. Some of my finest memories of my mother and I were during my younger years. Having nightmares, jumping out of my bed, running over to her bed, to feel secure, as we shared a bedroom on the third floor of my grandmother's house. My mother would spoil me rotten, and man did I love it, but being her only child had its ups and downs. I had tons of fun with my mother. She was funny, but subdued as well, until she would stand up in front of the church on

Sundays and sing her heart out for the love of God.

I remember every Sunday getting up listening to

Shirley Cesar blaring on the radio, as we got

dressed for Sunday service. My mom would get me

anything I asked for, but I don't remember her ever

having thoughtful conversations with me or telling

me I could be or do whatever I wanted to do in this

world. I recognize now, how those words of

positive affirmation really mean a lot in the long

run. Up until around eight years of age, my mother

kept me by her side at all times. This is when she

met my siblings' father, whom I felt changed the

entire scope of my mother's life. My mother's

decision to venture outside her normal routine has

always baffled me, because to this very day my

mother will not try anything outside of her comfort

zone.

This is a lady who had grown up in the fifth largest city in America, and has never been on the subway. She will not entertain the idea of boarding an airplane, which always frustrated me because in my mind I've always understood that I was going to be able to show my mother the world. But her deciding to break her church routine would have a long-term impact on the both of us for the rest of my life. At this time, she's now hanging out in the street and going to bars, which was way out of my mother's normal movements. My mother met my siblings' father, let's call him Harold, who to me was not the best thing to have happened to my mother because the day he walked into her life was the day I lost my mother. Yes, I know that may sound selfish, but it was a short-term thing that started off as an attempt to create a makeshift family that was short lived and I was never a real fan from the start. This would be a relationship that would last over thirty years but lost me in the process. I remember us living in an apartment up the street from my grandmother on the top floor above my aunt and her family. It went from the two of us living in this one-bedroom apartment, to this strange man now living with us who I was never formally introduced to; but there he was in our space and I hated every minute of it. My mother never had a conversation with me about him and as much as I tried to like him, I just was never a fan.

One of the primary reasons I didn't like him was because he wasn't my father. I think that's most little boys' impression because in the end nothing or nobody can replace your father, and because of my mother I showed him respect. My mother would get up and go to work and leave me with this man. He would take me out bike riding and so forth, now these activities did not last long. Because the next thing I know, I started seeing less of my mother. She ran the streets now, which was something I was not use to. The less I saw of my mother, the more I was back at my grandmother's house with no mother around. I'm asking my grandmother where my mother was and she would always make up an excuse as to where she was.

I feel in a lot of ways I've held a sense of resentment for my mother because of her leaving me for a man, but I never stopped loving her. I mean you're always going to LOVE mom no matter what, but there is a strong feeling of hurt that I think I've just understood how to let go and attempt to move past; I can't lie and say it didn't have negative effects on my life because it has. When my mother just abruptly stopped coming around I was left with my grandmother, Mozell Sutton. No matter the situation she always had my back. I remember one time my cousin Eddie and I was out being boys, doing what boys of our time did. One day we decided to climb a barbed wire gate and flip over it. Well, we did just that and when I flipped over it I let go of the wire and ripped the side of my thumb wide open on my left hand. Back then I had a real fear of blood so as soon as my cousin pointed it out I instantly freaked out and ran to my grandmother. My grandmother being the phenomenal grandmother she was, calmed me right down as only she knew how. She took a look at my hand, ran some cold water over it to slow the blood down. Then she told me to stay still as she made her way to the basement. When she returned, she had a spider web wrapped around the end of a broomstick. I'm like, *'grandma what are you about to do with that?'* She began to explain that when she was a kid in South Carolina black folks were

not allowed in the hospitals to get taken care of the

proper way, so when she had deep cuts her mother

would pack the it with a spider web. The spider web

would bond the skin together and keep it from

becoming infected. She packed my cut with spider

web and prayed over my hand afterward, to this day

I still have that scar and never had any issues or

infections with my hand via that scar.

My grandmother did the best she could until

she felt it was too much for her. She decided to send

me to my mother's older sister, who we use to live

above in our previous apartment. My aunt lived in

an area of Philly called Fern Rock with my uncle

and two of my female cousins. This was a life-

changing event, because now I've been forced to

leave what I knew and go to an entirely new

environment and school; and I still hadn't heard

from my mother. These moves truly made me feel lonely. I remember getting up some mornings looking at the front door hoping that my mother was going to ring the bell and say she was there to pick me up. This was a very, very, lonely period in my life; not knowing why my mother just threw me away like trash. She never took the time to check on me, and why was this man now more important to her than me? That she felt it was ok to walk away and leave me on my grandmother. I felt like I was consistently walking around in the dark looking for the light switch, but continuously being denied due to my lack of worthiness.

A lot of the time I felt out of place at my aunt's house, like I was taking up space. Being in this space and never hearing someone tell you *I love you* and *it's going to be all right* was very hard for me. My grandmother would send food stamps every month on my behalf. I remember having one pair of underwear for months and being too scared to tell anyone, plus I felt way too embarrassed to ever mention it to anyone. My shelter was my older sister Deanna who would come and get me from time-to-time and keep me for the weekend. It was something about my sister's very strong love for me that I felt every time I was in her presence; it was a sense of shelter and refuge. That helped with my loneliness I was struggling with daily, so I was comfortable telling her that I had one pair of underwear. I knew she would make sure I was ok in the end, even with her not knowing that I felt embarrassed. There were times that I wanted to ask her to keep me and take care of me, but never had the heart, plus she was only six years older than me. I was very young dealing with emotions that I had no idea how to express. Don't get me wrong I appreciate my aunt taking me into her home, as she could have told my grandmother NO!

Grandmothers are some of the most intuitive people on Earth for them to have not given birth to you, as their grandchild they somehow know how to become in tune with their grandkids as if they physically had you. My grandmother was so in tune with me that one-day I went to visit and spend the day with her at the house, we never had a conversation about my state of mind or feelings about my current situation, she just knew. As I was about to leave her house this day she said *'Richard, come here.'* So I am like *'yes grandma?'* She said, *'you're not happy at your aunt's house are you?'* I just shook my head no. She said *'fine no worries you stay here.'* She kept me, called my aunt and said *'I'm going to come get Richard's clothes.'* Now I'm sure they had an in-depth conversation around the matter but my young ears were not privy

to that conversation. I don't know I never went back

to my aunt's house, but was very appreciative that

she took me in and cared for me as her own.

CHAPTER FOUR: MOZELL SUTTON

Thus began my journey of being passed around the family like a half-smoked joint. Back at my grandmother's house not sure of what would be next, one thing that I was always confident about was that my grandmother would make sure I was safe, protected and loved. When I was younger, before my grandmother sent me to my mother's eldest sister, I attended Robert Fulton Elementary School. Picture day had come and I remember telling my grandmother that I had to take pictures the next day. She was surprised but said, '*no worries I will make sure you're dressed and ready to go for tomorrow.*' Well there was a small problem; I hadn't had a haircut. Let me tell you, in my younger years I did not have the best grade of hair, especially not to have had a haircut and take a picture. My hair would look horrible as my father once said *"you have nigger knots and beebee shots of little angry black men with their fists balled up."* So just imagine how I looked in this picture that I had taken in the fifth grade. When those pictures came back I was so upset because I looked so horrible, but my grandmother loved them. I swear I thought she was trying to torture me with a slow death. She hung the picture up and was giving copies to family and friends. I would never like to brush my hair or keep it groomed as needed, but after that picture it was never a problem again. As time passed and I was moving on to middle school, grandmother decided to make another call to reach out to my mother's other sister to see if she would be willing to carry the burden of allowing me to be a part of her household.

GENERATION X

Before I jump into another *pack- your –
bags- and -travel –moment*, let me just stop for a
second. Over my lifetime I have seen plenty of
people profess how much of a man they are, but
what I have learned is when you find the need to
solidify your manhood you're usually in the
struggle to figure it out. Imagine having plenty of
men around you but still no idea of what being a
man stands for or looks like. This concept of
manhood is talked about as if it comes with
instructions of *'how to'* when in reality, it's just a
concept misdirected by media and music;
particularly rap music. I dare to ask the question of
what manhood really is to most people. I'm almost
sure that seeing consistency in the reply would be
like seeing a politician follow through on what they

actually campaign on while running for office. One of the biggest challenges, I believe, is that most young black males have an understanding that the definition of manhood is self-love. Then again, how could they if that's been a misplaced word rarely used or even heard coming from a man to a boy as a word of comfort and confirmation?

I grew up in the generation where we were always informed to suck it up. That little boys don't cry because that makes you look like a punk. Showing signs of weakness was usually not tolerated, but this is also the era of single black women trying their best to raise young boys to become men to the best of their ability. Why, because in the 70's and 80's the black man was missing from the family structure due to drugs, and mass incarceration. A lot of times, in my early twenties and thirties, I struggled with understanding how I should carry myself, as well as what I wanted

people to think of me as a man, or what I thought

was a man. The struggle with identifying the

concept and reality of what being a man is, has such

an impact on a young boy; particularly entering into

your teen years because at this point you now have

the spark to engage into talking to little girls. Not

realizing your level of dysfunction to understand

this species, called girls, who eventually become

women; this could be one of the critical pieces to

the fear of becoming man. I don't think there is

truly a science to understanding a woman. To never

have had someone sit you down to discuss your

interactions with little girls, the importance of the

respect you should show them, and their importance

to us long term in life is a problem. I believe that

there should always be a conversation with a young

boy about how he should interact with, treat, and

deal with a young lady. A young boy should also realize this is seen through how he treats and respects his mother.

I think about my understanding growing up around relationships with women and how I struggled with loyalty and commitment to one woman. Even though I was never taught to dog women out or treat them less than Queens, I would have to be honest with my reality and how I struggled in this area of my life. Women and manhood is another layer in this struggle of misleading cultural blindness in manhood.

CHAPTER FIVE: EDUCATIONAL CHALLENGES

Let's discuss how labels play a part in confidence and struggle in this search for manhood. In my educational career there were moments of pure doubt with less confidence to believe that I was capable to even compete or have the smarts. I still struggle with a lack of confidence in my intelligence from time-to-time. When I hear people say how smart I am, subconsciously I find myself thinking, *damn who would have ever thought this would be you*? Hell, who would have ever thought that I would be willing to tell my story in book form, to make an effort to let another young brother know it's all possible? Let's take a journey through my educational background to understand why I've felt this way, and how it plays into the man I have become.

To say the least, it is always a challenge when I take the opportunity to flash back on my childhood and my education.

I remember as a young child attending a catholic elementary school for one year. I have a vague memory of that year as far as education, and I don't remember there being a focus or conversation around my educational growth. The craziest part, is my biggest memory of this particular catholic school is a young lady named Ebony, who I had the biggest crush on that year. She would always have my attention because I thought she was the most beautiful girl in my class. She was short with wavy black hair, dark bronze skin that was very soft, and I remember her grandmother picking her up from school each day. After I left that school, I cannot recall thinking about Ebony any more. I know, I know; you're like what does that have to do with anything? It's a critical aspect because out of an entire year of receiving an education, I don't recall the nuns of the school really investing into my educational progress. I remember them not allowing me back the following year, so I ended up back in the Philadelphia public school system, with a label. That year I attended Robert Fulton Elementary School and being in Mrs. Rose's class. Her class was where I felt that she cared a little more about my learning capabilities. At this time I hadn't yet been labeled "special education/learning disability (LD)". I was still considered normal, I guess, in those terms of not having a label as a young black male. I think at that time I had to have been in about the third or fourth grade. I had no real clue of the struggles I was having in school at that time but it wasn't really due to me being incapable of doing the work—I would say really more to outside factors at that time that were way out of my control as child.

One of the primary things I remember as a child, was that I missed a lot of school being raised by a single parent mother who had not graduated from high school herself. I believe that played a part as to how seriously my mother took education. I was my mother's only child, at the time. I can't tell you why I missed so much school at such a young age and very critical time in my educational career. I remember there being issues with the school due to my absenteeism, it would improve for a while then fall back to me missing school. This period of time is very critical because I feel this played a big part in me being labeled special education/learning disability in the fifth grade. It wasn't helping my cause missing so much school during this time because I was taking reading classes to improve my struggle in reading. The funny thing is, I did miss a lot of school but was still pushed through the system to my next grade, even though there was no way I was ready to move on due to my high absenteeism. This was way before George Bush's No Child Left Behind legislation!

I was still attending Robert Fulton but my grandmother felt she was not the best fit for me. When I started sixth grade she decided to send me to my mother's eldest sister's house to be raised; here I started Howe Elementary School.

I remember my first day of class in this school, it didn't help that everything was foreign to me due to an entirely new environment both personally and educationally. Walking into this classroom seeing only five students, in my mind wasn't right, but I had no choice or say-so in the matter whatsoever. It's a very helpless feeling that I am unable to articulate. At times, I find this feeling to be a driving force in me and I find myself in situations that drive me to mentally revisit that place and time in my childhood. I spent one year at Howe because it only went to the sixth grade, but it was a very interesting year. I spent the year sitting in a class getting straight "A's" and "B's" on my report card, but was never asked is there something deeper to my success. I remember always being uncomfortable in the class because all of the other students would stare at us as if we were different. The craziest thing is, I was unaware that I was labeled at this time, but knew that my class looked different in terms of the number of students and classmates in the other classes. I found out that my class and the work was really different than that of my peers while standing in the schoolyard talking to a friend who was not in my class. He asked me about something that they were learning at that time and I had no clue nor if it was something that we were learning. When we returned to class that day, I remember asking my teacher Mrs. Silverstine about it and she informed me that they were a more advanced class and our class was on a slower track on the learning path, which is why we were in a special education class.

To be honest, the impact of being labeled at that time was not as harsh because I brushed it off in an attempt to mask my embarrassment. The label was more of an issue when we were at recess one day and a few kids starting picking with a classmate and myself, as they called us LD and stupid. We were playing wall ball and talking trash at the same time. Each of us was cracking momma jokes when one of the kids took it personal. He decided to hone

in on a classmate and I, telling everyone that we

were in special education classes. The anger I felt

from the embarrassment, caused me to want to

fight. We were separated by other classmates,

stopping us from fighting. Due to the

embarrassment, I was upset for the rest of the day.

Kids are harsh; they have no true understanding of

the impact of words because they're being kids, but

when you're on the receiving end of those harsh

words it can be a feeling of emptiness and failure.

The disappointment of wondering if you are even

smart enough or able to keep up with your peers.

Yeah, I can say that now as a 39-year-old

grown man, but back then it bothered me a lot. It

didn't bother me because it was a form of being

picked on, or in today's terms bullying, but more of

am I less intelligent than that of my peers who are

not sitting in this class of eight students? If you were to ask my take on the education that I was receiving, I would have to say nothing truly impressive. As I stated, I was getting "A's" and "B's" so everyone was impressed by my grades. I feel your parents or guardians should be overly involved in your education and how much it is, or isn't challenging you. I say that because I never felt like I was challenged so the work was nothing of substance. You may be thinking: *why would he say that? He was too young to even judge it,* but I'm currently speaking from the eyes of a grown man. The rest of that year, I stuck to the script since I had already been doing it; for that entire year I carried a "B" average as a sixth grader in special education classes. My teacher at the time was ok, but I can't recall her name; we have to remember that year was a lot of adjustments for me with my living situation having its ups and downs to say the least. But, honestly how many real problems can a ten-year-old have?

I spent that year doing a lot of adjusting to home, school, and making friends in my new neighborhood. I don't remember ever being one that had great study habits, nor had I ever learned the art of good study habits when it came to my schoolwork. Howe was my true introduction to understanding that I was sitting in a class that made me different from all the other kids, but had not been explained as to why I was different. My grandmother felt living with her would be a better fit than my current situation with my eldest aunt. I never realize how much change I had endured during my childhood, but I guess it's because all of my change was within family. I'm appreciative that I wasn't lost to the system, that was largely due to my grandmother being so present in my life; which this made my journey with my education a little easier.

Well, on to middle school where I attended Pickett Middle School, which at the time was one of the roughest schools in my neighborhood. Pickett was different because we had different color-coded house in the school, in which I found a little intimidating. We had the houses coded to the particular grade in which you were in; I was in the red house. These particular classes again ostracized you from the rest of the student population in as how you were learning, but I also had to deal with the fact that again I was in these particular classes that stood out from those of the rest of my peers. To be honest just as it was in elementary school, I felt different from the rest of my friends and not in a good way. That always bothered me, but I never truly addressed it. Once again, I was forced to sit in these classes with the same people for an entire eight hours and the only time we changed classes was to go to gym. Again, my first year there I made myself stay in line with what was given and asked no questions.

I remember my second year, I had a science teacher by the name of Ms. Stevens. I remember her because she was very hard on us and gave us no breaks. She would always say *"the world won't be easy on you so why should I?"* I never forgot her because she had hazel brown eyes and was very attractive, but beside her physical features, she made sure we were aware that she cared about us and felt that it was critical that we took our education seriously. I find it crazy that through my younger educational career I can count on one hand the number of teachers that I remember who really cared and showed that they cared about us as students. One thing I remember most about Ms. Stevens, was she never treated us like kids who were labeled as special education/learning disability; something about her just wouldn't subscribe to that mindset. She was the one who always made us feel normal in her class, and I believe a big part of that was just in the way she would teach us. Everyone else treated us as if we were incapable of learning on a higher level. I always respected Ms. Stevens for that because she made me feel like I had no learning issues while attending her class. Ms. Stevens displayed her passion for teaching with every effort and encounter I had with her. This to me made a very big difference in how I felt every time I was in her science class. I was so intrigued by Ms. Stevens, she made learning about science fun, not that science had become my favorite subject, but being in her presence became my empowerment.

Middle school in and of itself, was a rollercoaster ride of emotions and adjustments because it introduced more challenges, coupled with being a preteen and puberty. Puberty is another conversation itself; it makes it harder to deal with not having a man that you could discuss these changes that you have to now face with your body. The life of a middle school kid and being in classes that were different from your friends, coupled with no one ever explaining to you why, could have a long-term effect. I feel I happened to have lucked-up. I didn't allow the fact that I was already labeled not to win, to kill my drive. That could be up for argument!

Growing up there was a clear difference in how education was perceived on my mother's side of the family verses my father's side of the family. I can't really say the family, more of how my mother's focus was when it came to my education. At times, it didn't seem as important to her as it did to my father when I was around his house. He played no games with my education nor was missing school an option. As I moved on to live with my Aunt Rochelle she would go to my parent-teacher meetings and so forth. By then, the damage of being in these classes had already been engraved but let me not jump ahead too much. Living with my Aunt Rochelle was a little more of a game changer, because she actually stayed on top of me and it was no games when report card time rolled around. She never missed an opportunity to go up to the school to get my report card and speak to my teachers about my behavior and grades; let my grades not be on point- punishment was inevitable!

Going back to the difference of perception of education between my two families.   A lot of times when I would go see my father, it was because he lived with my grandmother and three of my uncles. When I would stay over my grandmother's house during a school week it was critical that I had no options to play, talk on the phone, or watch television. It was a very strict rule that you sat at the kitchen table and did your homework, and you were not allowed to leave that kitchen table until you were finished. The majority of the time, my father was never around for these interactions as he would be in the streets. It would be left to my Uncle Barnes to police my other cousins that would be over that week and myself.

Honestly, those were the times that I had someone at home fully invested in my education, and gaining an understanding of what I learned for the day. Uncle Barnes was a real drill sergeant and would ride our backs until we completed our homework and could prove to him that we understood what we completed. Math was never really my strongest subject and I would always struggle in math really bad (go figure I grow up and become a manager of a bank). One evening while doing my homework, I really struggled while completing my math. My uncle was hard on me, not letting up until I got the lesson. It really made me feel stupid and inadequate. I remember saying that I was in LD classes because I was not smart, my uncle wasn't trying to hear that. He said to stop making excuses as to why I couldn't get the work done. That was such a pivotal moment in my life because that was such a rough day, that even as I write this I can visualize it very well. I believe it's because I had such a hard time but my family was not letting me make excuses as to why I couldn't,

but I wanted to give up.

This same situation has to be one of the

finest memories in my entire life of my father. I

guess my uncle had a conversation with my father

when he decided to come in the house that night

about my struggles, and what he dealt with that

evening trying to help me complete the math

portion of my homework. I remember my father

coming into the room to wake me and discuss what

my issues were. During the conversation, I made the

mistake of calling myself "stupid" in his presence.

Well allow me to tell you what a mistake that was! I

remember him grabbing me really tight by my arms

pulling me close to him; he looked me in my eyes

and said in a very stern and aggressive voice *"if I

ever hear you call yourself stupid again, I'm going

to whip your ass!"* He proceeded to tell me that

there was nothing about me that was stupid and that I should never take an opportunity to degrade myself, as society will look for every opportunity to do that for me. *"Don't give anyone the power to see you as less than."* This coming from a man who had never raised his voice at me, nor put his hands on me in my life. Needless to say, I was petrified after that encounter. To this very day, I have never used that word in reference to myself. My father didn't do much for me in my life, but that situation was a game-changer for my life, and how I perceive what I thought and how I felt about myself both educationally and emotionally. I believe that single situation saved my life as far education goes. After this experience with my father, I still struggled with my confidence as far as my education but I never forgot, because every time I doubted myself I could hear his voice and picture his facial expression speaking those words to me. That memory would give me that push I needed to continue in my doubt I would have of myself in educational challenges.

Whoever decides to come up with these labels for kids, never take the opportunity to look at the overall impact that these labels can have on a child's self-esteem, development of social skills, and communication skills. To me, being labeled as learning disabled says I'm incapable of learning and lack the developmental aspects of those of my peers. With the challenges that black males already have to face from day one of leaving their mother's womb, this to me says: let's kill any hopes and dreams that this young child may have by subliminally, letting him know that the system doesn't care to find out about your learning styles. It's much easier to label you and plant the seed that you are unable to learn in the traditional manner.

When these labels are applied how many parents really do their due diligence to see if it is indeed the right fit for their child's learning style? All I'm saying is, if no one is willing to fight for you to find out why these labels are being placed on you, would you have any belief in yourself if they were already telling you that you're different? Nothing about this difference is speaking positivity to who you are or what you could become.

One of the biggest things I've always struggled with was that I felt no one felt the need to fight for me or helped me understand why I was placed in those classes. Okay, I've completed middle school and now I am moving on to high school; Germantown High School, September of 1990. Boy did I have so many mixed emotions, moving on once again, while this time my home life had become a lot more stable due to my Aunt

Rochelle. Germantown High School was our neighborhood school, which you would automatically be sent to after completing Clarence E. Pickett Middle School, unless your parents had applied or had plans of sending you to another high school. Which in my case wasn't the situation, but Germantown had a lot of family history so I really didn't mind; my father, older brother, aunt, uncle, mother and cousins had all attended the school. I was now a freshman at a very rough neighborhood school. I kept thinking about the start of school that summer prior to September. Would I have to fight a lot from being picked on for being in special education classes and would it be as obvious as it was when I was in middle school that I was in these classes?

Well, that summer seemed to have flown past so fast and I was very nervous as to what this experience was going to be. I think I was even more nervous about my class situation, how difficult the experience was going to be, and what type of impact it would have. To me this was do or die, it had been years since I heard someone tell me *you're not stupid, you're very smart, and can accomplish anything!* Now that I'm thinking about it, no one has ever told me that I could accomplish anything I put my mind to, outside of the conversation with my father around calling myself stupid. When it came to my education, not much positive reinforcement was given for the sake of my self-confidence. I believe I lucked-up in a lot of ways because I carried myself with a lot of confidence which made me a little harder to read when it came to a few of my struggles in school. It really was a defense mechanism to hide the fact that I was embarrassed that I was in these classes. I would have to find a way to play off the fact that I was going in these special education classes.

It was obvious that these classes were special education because the placement in which the rooms were located in the building. They were always at the end of the hall or around the corner from the other classes. Allow me to put this in perspective for you: Germantown was a very big school with three floors and two wings on both the north and south side of the building. A lot of times my classes were on or close to these wings in the building and it would stand out because all of the other kids were not coming back that far to attend class. It was noticeable but I proceeded to do what I needed to do and did not allow it to bother me, or at least I pretended not to allow it to bother me. I do believe what kept me from being ridiculed and picked on was my personality and the way in which

I carried myself. I mean to this day very few of my classmates from high school are aware that I was in special education classes and was labeled learning disability. I must add that I also owe a great deal of gratitude to my ninth-grade science teacher (special education).

Quality teachers are critical to a child's education; quality in a teacher who understands their purpose, the impact they can and will have on a child's life, the method in which they deliver their message, and their will to recognize a child's true potential. Teachers may spend more hours with a child than an actual parent because of the amount of time a child spends in school during the course of a day, week and school year. In high school, I was lucky enough to have had the opportunity to come across three teachers who impacted my life in a very profound way. It was all in the manner in which they spoke to me and showed they cared about me. My ninth-grade science teacher Mr. Kline would be the one to change my educational blueprint. While attending his class for the majority of my ninth-grade year, I remember one Monday morning leaving his room and Mr. Kline stops me and proceeds to ask me, *"Richard why are you in my class, and do you find my work to be easy?"* I respond, *"I'm not sure Mr. Kline, I just get the work done as you give it to us."* Without hesitation he says to me, *"I don't believe you need to be in my class and I'm going to speak to a few of your other teachers and I'll get back to you."*

Approximately two weeks later I arrived to Mr. Kline's class, my first class of the day, and as I attempted to walk into his room he stopped me at the door. *"You're no longer in my class Richard!"* As I am taken aback by this statement I ask, *"what exactly do you mean Mr. Kline, did I do something*

wrong?" Mr. Kline says, *"remember our brief*

conversation two weeks ago and I asked you how

you felt about the work I was giving you?" *"Yes! I*

remember that conversation sir." *"Well I have had*

you removed from all your special education

classes except math, and that's only because your

teacher wouldn't sign off on the paperwork. But the

good news is everyone else did so you are no longer

in these classes."

It was one of the best feelings of my life; it

immediately boosted my academic confidence

because this said that I wasn't stupid, and that I

wasn't incapable of learning the same information

my friends were learning. That day was such a high

for me but an immediate fear for a second. The fear,

because now I was going to be in class with my

friends, getting the same work they were receiving,

and wondering could I really keep up after not getting everything they were getting by being labeled and placed in special education classes? I did fine in the change of classes. I have to admit I was blessed and had some very good teachers, like my English teacher Mrs. Bagley, science teacher Mr. Kellum, communications teacher Mr. Ramsey who I would say were all vital in my success in high school and lifting my confidence. They never allowed me to say *I can't,* nor would they make themselves unavailable if I needed assistance or understanding.

Mrs. Bagley was my English teacher who opened my eyes to Shakespeare and reading. I didn't appreciate it then, but I love it now as I read more now than I've ever have. I believe I beat the odds and I say that because not only did I achieve graduating high school, I also went on to attend

Shaw University in Raleigh, North Carolina.

According to the so-called data, I wasn't supposed

to do any of this.

CHAPTER SIX: MIGHTY SHAW UNIVERSITY

I would have to admit attending Shaw was one of the best moves I've ever made. I would also have to admit that I wasn't truly ready for what I had walked into as far as education. I can't say that I struggled, but I was not truly ready for the discipline it takes to be successful in college. I remember the day I arrived to school with my Aunt Rochelle and Uncle Lestor. When we arrived on campus there were these two buildings, which looked like the projects back in Philly. My aunt looked at me and said, *"are you sure you want to stay here?"* Now she's asking this to an eighteen-year-old whose hormones were all out of control. As she's asking me this I see this young lady walk out of the girls' dorm with this jet-black long hair and very pretty face; she almost looked Asian. I looked back at my aunt and said, *"Oh! Yes, I'll be just fine here."*

The truth is, my focus was not where it needed to be, I spent three years at this awesome university and met some really cool people, and I still dropped out. My focus was not clear and it was one of the reasons why was I was not respecting the importance of my education. I had this dream of becoming a model and actor, so I dropped out and attended a modeling school in Raleigh. To this day I can't tell you why I felt that was more important than finishing my education. The funny thing is, I was the first person on my mother's side of the family, as far as I know, to even attend college. I swear, my focus back then was in all the wrong places. The awesome thing is, even though I didn't graduate, my circle from Shaw still supports me to this very day, even though I dropped out. Attending Shaw also helped to build character within myself as well as forge my communication skills.

Here's what is even crazier about it all: since my college years, a few of my family members have since attended and completed college. My Aunt Rochelle; my cousin who is currently working on his PhD, this is so crazy to me because he's my little big cousin and I'm super proud of him; his little sister (they both are my Aunt Rochelle's kids). My older sister Deanna has her master's degree and my little sister Shana has her Bachelor's degree. Eventually, I will at some point return to finish my degree in business management so it's not something I started and just didn't finish.

CHAPTER SEVEN: A DIFFERENT WORLD

When I think about attending college there was never a time anyone sat me down and even discussed the option of going to college. I had just happened to have an associate during my high school years with whom I spent a lot of time with and spoke about college; to be honest he was the only one to have ever mentioned college to me outside of watching *A Different World* every Thursday night after *The Cosby Show*. It was never a discussion around my house. Here's the irony in it all: I ended up going to college and he never applied for college. I always find it crazy, but I looked at it as it may have been his sole purpose of being in my life at that time and the reason I made it to college.

I truly believe all our lives have purpose. I believe a part of my purpose is to tell my story in order to show some young black male right now who's ready to give up, has been labeled by the education system, and/or feels defeated before he even has the opportunity to imagine a bright future; that it's possible. "…Anything the mind can conceive the mind can achieve," Napoleon Hill. This is a concept that has to be stressed to these young boys so they can feel they have a chance. My grandmother would not allow me to soak in the pity of underperforming, even when I struggled in my younger years with reading. She was a pastor and would always have my cousins and I in her church in the basement of her house. She would make me stand up and read the Bible in front of everyone, even though I was not the best reader, but

I appreciate her for that because I believe that helped improve my reading ability very much.

Yes! This 39-year-old African American male has beaten the odds; not only overcoming that which I wasn't supposed to, but remember they left me in special education classes for math. I still ended up in the financial industry becoming a Branch Manager remaining in the industry for a little over ten years; now I'm an Entrepreneur and Inspirational Speaker. There cannot be limitations set on young boys' lives, while I believe I am one of many who have beaten the odds I know there are even more who haven't. The cards are already being stacked against us. That's why I find it essential for teachers who care and are passionate about teaching to remain active in the education system. I salute those teachers who are driven by the effective and affective change that they may never get to see, but will emotionally be a part of, as was my teachers. In the end, I say let's stop with the labels and adjust the art of learning to fit that of our children. Let's empower them to believe, without questioning whether they can achieve the highest of heights in life, especially if they're willing to put in the work and do what's required. That was not the message I was receiving in my early years of learning, not from home or school.

CHAPTER EIGHT: SELF-DOUBT

As I think about my life as a young black male growing up in the inner city of Philadelphia, I always had dreams of being more than my circumstances and my struggle to overcome my self-doubt and loneliness. I remember back in my mid-twenties my aunt who has been more like my mother over the years said to me, *"nephew I hope you find whatever it is your looking for."* That statement has always bothered me and I don't believe there was malicious intent behind it. I think she was watching me while I was in search of who I was or trying to become, but had no real advice for me so she said what came to her mind. As I look back at that situation it now makes sense to me; she was a concerned mother watching her nephew/son in search of manhood. But she wasn't a man nor has she ever been a black man, she was trying as only a mother figure would in showing her thoughts and love.

Growing up there were a lot of women in my life from my mother, grandmother, big sister, and aunts who raised me. It would also be a lie to say I didn't have men in my life, because I truly did, even though they may have not been active or even always present. There were no soft men in my family. They showed me a lot indirectly. Some of them were into selling drugs and some were using drugs heavily, so I understood the effects of both sides.

CHAPTER NINE: SUPERMAN

I am a very observant person and have always been since I was a kid. I watched how my father and uncles move about when they would have me hang out with them as a kid. They all had their flaws, but they were all stand up men in their own right. I watched the devastating impact of drugs on the men in my family. Growing up, one of my favorite uncles could do no wrong in my eyes. He was my mother's brother and when I tell you I admire my uncle, words could not capture my admiration for this man. As a young buck, I remember my uncle coming home from the military—he served in the United States Army. Allow me to give you a brief description of my uncle. He was about 5'11 with a chiseled body. He would get up very early in the morning, take three eggs crack them into a glass in swallow them, then go running; he would take me with him. I would get tired and end up on his shoulders as he continued to run with me hoisted up on his shoulders.

My uncle was a very good-looking man. It was always amazing to me how women responded to him. Man look, some of the most beautiful women would come through looking for my uncle and he would always look cool, calm, and collected; they would be in awe. He also had one of the most beautiful personalities he would do almost anything to help anyone. My uncle was also affectionately referred to as *Tweety Bird*. My aunt tells me he received this nickname because he reminded everyone of "Tweety Bird" from the Warner Brothers Looney Tunes cartoon. He was very skilled as a bricklayer. I would be in awe as I watched him replace the concrete at my grandmother's house. When he finished the front of the house looked brand new.

He was a man's man in so many ways, I recall swinging out with my uncle as I would always do every chance he would allow. There was this one time he had me with over his girlfriend's house on was a hot summer night. Everyone was out on the block like normal in the hood back in the 80's; there were a bunch of guys playing tackle football on the street. They were all older than me, but I didn't care and wanted to play. I asked my uncle and he said *"sure go head let me see what you look like out there."* So I jumped out there and started having so much fun until everything went left real fast. One of the guys threw the football to one of his teammates and I attempted to intercept the ball, but remember we are playing on the streets in the hood where there are broken bottles, trash, and Philly potholes; such an awesome combination. I go to grab the ball, slipped, and slid on my knees in a bunch of broken glass. The look on my uncle's face was calm, cool, and collected to keep me from freaking out. He grabbed me, picked me up, and we were on our way back to my grandmother's house. I remember my uncle telling me *"keep calm, don't cry, you're a big boy, I got you, and we don't want your mother and your grandmother to find out."*

He always had a way of being so smooth in his movement and keeping me calm but my knee would not stop bleeding, as soon as we walked in the house my grandmother was sitting there like she already knew there was something wrong. She always did, but because my favorite uncle said *play it cool*, I PLAYED along with everything he told me to do. The crazy part is, I still have the scar on my left knee to this very day. I admire him very

much; he was also a Golden Gloves boxer while in

the military. He was so good, yet many people

feared my uncle. He had people stab him and

attempt to jump him; it was crazy. His girlfriend's

brothers were scared of him. They had a major

falling out and one of her brothers called himself

stepping to my uncle. Now my uncle would never

put his hands on a woman, but her brother felt that

he should not have been arguing with their sister

and raising his voice. One of her brothers decided

he needed to check my uncle and let him know that

arguing with his sister wasn't the best move. This

was such a bad decision on his part, because for

some reason he decided to swing on my uncle so,

my uncle knocked him out in the middle of the

street. I mentioned my uncle was already feared

and respected, but he never walked around with his

chest out like he was the baddest man in the hood; but he also didn't play when it came to his family and his safety.

A few days later, the same dude my uncle knocked out snuck up on him and stabbed him in his kidney. This almost killed him, which turned into a family war between my family and his girlfriend's family. This was a crazy period in my life because I watched my aunts and uncles tear fire to the hood for about a week. After that incident I always felt like my uncle was never the same. He would go on to be stabbed two more times by different people because they were scared to fight him due to how deadly he was with his hands. I tell this story of my Uncle *Tweety Bird* because he was strong on so many levels and just like my father I really admired him. As I got older, we drifted apart because he started using drugs.

Drugs took over my hero and slowly destroyed him so bad that I can recall a time sitting at the traffic light and he walked past. He looked me in the eye and didn't recognize me. My heart broke and tears filled my eyes because I had now become totally disconnected from one of my heroes, but how does this happen? How does Superman become mortal?

I never had anyone sit me down and discuss becoming a man or the struggles of becoming a black man, but I swear I had glimpses of it in so many ways from my uncles. Now they may not have been what society depicts as real men, but to me they all were, in their own way, but fell victim to bad choices. In the hood/urban Philadelphia, drugs are so prevalent that it's in the fabric of our neighborhoods. Drugs have taken a toll on our families in the inner city and my uncles were no different, but my uncle Bird was truly like

Superman in a lot of ways. Many times the streets

and his decisions tried to claim his life, but

somehow he would bounce back. One time, he

overdosed on drugs and flat lined. As the doctor

was about to pronounce him dead, my uncle opened

his eyes and grabbed the nurse's arm. That

happened at least three different times, and no I'm

not trying to sensationalize this story in any manner.

My uncle was a very different type of man who for

some reason God would not let him leave this Earth

on his terms. A year ago he finally checked out, it

took me a full twenty-four hours for it to actually

set in because in my mind, Superman couldn't die.

Death had knocked at his door so many other times

but was denied access. Uncle Bird had so many

great qualities about him as a person and as man,

but I feel he never made the decision to stand fully

in his greatness for whatever reason; he and my

father were a lot alike in so many ways. I witnessed

two potentially great black men not accept their

greatness, but in the end they indirectly taught me

so many life lessons. I pray that I become half the

man they both were and achieve the greatness they

both were unsuccessful in achieving.

MANHOOD

Manhood is an ever-evolving process that I think is so much bigger than society's perception of what they think it should be. It's so much bigger than material possessions. A man is one who grows from his mistakes, and is always willing to learn because he understands that a real man doesn't stop learning until he dies. He's ever-evolving into who he becomes, while never becoming stagnant in his growth. He knows that how many women he has sex with is so far from what a real man is, and understands that is the mentality of a boy trying to figure out his way. Manhood is truth and understanding; knowing that you have to handle your business even when you don't feel like it, or being capable of walking away from a situation that isn't conducive to your growth. Manhood is knowing when to ask for help and not allowing your pride to deceive you into believing otherwise; modeling the attributes of those men you feel are what you could see yourself becoming in the future.

This manhood thing plays such a big part in the moves we make. One thing I always believe we struggle with in the black community, is marriage, and the lack thereof due to the mass incarceration that has plagued our communities for decades. We 70's babies were directly impacted by the drug culture and the breakdown of the black family. While growing up, my friends at the time, nor myself, had come from two parent homes. Most of us were raised by single parent women who were trying to figure it out and make their way with government assistance at the helm of our households. Now don't get me wrong, that government cheese that came in the long brown box was some of the best cheeses I've ever tasted to this very day. Shit, say what you want, but that cheese made the best cheese eggs, grilled cheese sandwiches, and cheese grits, I swear. Now if you were fortunate enough to have not had government cheese in your house you don't know what you were missing.

CHAPTER TEN: THE COSBY SHOW

Ghetto life wasn't always horrible. I promise you it teaches you some key survival skills, but back to the topic at hand. I believe having the opportunity to experience seeing a successful marriage makes a difference in how you engage women and your mindset towards relationships. Now I'm no psychiatrist, but I do believe it makes a difference in a young boy's mind in how he deals with a young lady, as we usually model what we see. When you've seen how your father treated your mother and the things he did to make her feel happy and secure it also makes you desire that type of relationship.

As a black male growing up in urban America, marriage isn't something that's discussed or even on our agenda as a future goal. But it would be ill of me to say *all* because I'm not in the position to speak for the masses, I'll say from my experience and the friends that I had growing up. I don't ever remember it being a part of any conversations we ever engaged in. The change came with *The Cosby Show*. Why you ask? Despite whatever your thoughts may be about Mr. Cosby today, he gave a lot of us urban youth hope for a family life, career options and college. *The Cosby Show* sparked possibilities for those of us that had grown up without a father figure in our life. For me, knowing Bill Cosby was from the neighborhood I grew up in, and attended the same high school I attended, made it seem even more possible for someone like myself. Watching *The Cosby Show* inspired me to go to college and I believe inspired us urban youth without father figures. I was unaware there were historical black colleges and universities prior to *The Cosby Show*. I believe *The Cosby Show* truly gave us urban youth hope.

CHAPTER ELEVEN: MAY I HAVE YOUR DAUGHTER'S HAND IN MARRIAGE?

Let's discuss my attempt at marriage, and how I failed horribly at it, but learned a lot. I truly feel getting married was, as my aunt says, being in search of that thing she would say I was looking for but this time I think it had relevance in some ways. My ex-wife was a southern girl born and raised in Richmond, Virginia. She was very close with her family. They interacted a lot, and to me that was something I didn't have and thought that it would be great for me, but I was wrong. Let me first give a little backdrop on how my ex-wife and I came to be. She and I both attended Shaw University in Raleigh, North Carolina. We knew each other in college, years later I'm back home in Philly. It's now the new boom of social media; at that time, it was *MySpace* and I was adamant about not getting on it. But my little cousin Sheena decided that she

wanted to make a profile for me so, she created one

for me and made it active.

Well after only being on the site for a few

days my now ex-wife reached out to me. She and I

started talking and it went from a talking via

MySpace to the phone every day for hours at a time.

This was odd to me as I wasn't looking for a

relationship, but to me she was everything and

totally different from Philly women. In my mind, I

felt like I had hit a goldmine. Man when I tell you I

was on cloud nine it just felt like life was going so

well for me. I just closed on my first house at the

age of 30. This was huge because I closed on my

first house on Friday 13, 2007, on my 30th birthday.

The feeling of accomplishment was one of the best

feelings of my life. So now I have a new house, a

new car, and this woman who lives four hours away

from me. Nothing could stop me now because I was in total happiness.

The plan was for her to relocate to Philly and I had everything to hold us down while she found work here. After her son's father had gotten wind of her happiness and that she was about to relocate, he decided to take her to court and stop her move. This left me with a major decision to make: should I walk away from the situation or step outside of my comfort zone and take a chance on this so-called love thing? I remember having a conversation with one of my favorite cousins in the world, Angie. I discussed my thoughts about my relationship situation with her. I was seeking her advice and she said, *"look, home is called home for a reason so if it doesn't work you can always come home."* To be honest, she gave me the true courage to take the leap and move to Richmond, and for the first time I think I stepped outside of my comfort zone.

Fast-forward a few months later I packed my stuff into a U-HAUL, my entire new house, and jumped on 95 South with all types of thoughts on my mind; but I was in love at the time and just knew I was making the best move for her and me. I made this move and we were married September 9, 2009 with complete ignorance of what I was getting myself into; nor did she. Let me say this, my ex-wife in so many ways was an awesome wife, but we were not ready for the challenges of marriage. I wasn't ready for the adjustment of being in a place like Richmond, nor was I ready for marriage to completely be honest. I bring up my marriage not to discuss my ex-wife but to discuss my struggles as a man in a marriage that in hindsight I was not ready for. I struggled so much in Richmond emotionally, financially, and spiritually that it hindered my growth with my ex-wife, as my unhappiness was apparent.

My ex-wife started to take notice and she made attempts to go out of her way to make me happy, but I was so far gone at times that it was pointless. It didn't help that we also had major differences in how we viewed our goals for the marriage financially; our most critical component of our relationship. We struggled with our communication, you never realize how critical it is that you and your spouse have a fairly good grasp on how to effectively communicate but even more importantly be able to also listen effectively.

Fear of becoming man is truly in question as you think you're already a man in your mind, but there is a different level of manhood because it's no longer just you. Now you're responsible for another man's daughter. You decided to ask him could you marry her and he's now entrusted her to you, so you have to do your best to be man of your word to the very best of your ability. I wasn't all the man I could have or should have been, and yes there were some pressing issues at times that I allowed myself to not grow through.

A part of manhood is allowing oneself to grow even in the most uncomfortable situations. The one thing I understand now, is that you have to be willing to fight for your marriage, and also understand that as much as you're willing to stand in the enjoyment of the good times, you have to be willing to stand just as hard during the down times. It's not always going to be easy and those are the times that should draw you two closer to one another in the depths of the struggle.

One of the pluses that I gained as an experience from my marriage was the relationship with my father-in-law and the lessons that I gained from him. It was always funny to me when my mother-in-law would say how much I reminded her of Mr. Tommy Evans Jr. (her husband), but I never could see it. I would always try to help him out because he had back issues from over the years, though he would rarely ever complain he would still try to do strenuous activities as if he had no issues. My respect for him was huge; this is a man that has a 'never say die' type of attitude. What was most important to me, was that he was a man of very strong character and a man of his word, a true stand up king. He and I would sit around and have conversations here and there.

Pop, as I would affectionately call him was a lot like a father figure to me in so many ways. I recall when he allowed me to cook on his grill, my mother in law, ex-wife and I were all super surprised, because this man doesn't allow anyone to touch his grill. Now I'm thinking to myself this is a monumental moment and I was honored. My father-in-law is a man of very few words but through my journey into manhood I was blessed to have this man be a part of it, and I always enjoyed being in his company. He is such an awesome cook; man let me tell you about one of my favorite meals that he would make: stuffed peppers. My mouth would water when Pops would cook these stuffed peppers, and the presentation of them was so awesome.

Pops showed me so much more, and one truly memorable moment I had with my father-in-law was when my ex-wife and I had a major falling out; over what I couldn't tell you. She decided to pull her family into our drama. Her family including

my father-in-law went to my house and removed all

of my ex-wife's belongings as well as my stepson's.

I come home to an empty house, no wife, no

stepson and none of their belongings. I was a little

hurt but didn't care because at that time I was in my

feelings still, and fed up with the situation entirely.

Sidebar: my father-in-law and I had a conversation

when I first approached him and ask for his

permission to marry his daughter. During that

conversation he said to me *"son as long as you*

never put your hands on my daughter, I will never

get in the middle of your marriage to my daughter."

As a man you have to respect that request.

Well, after being involved in the removal of

my ex-wife's belongings he came to me and

apologized for participating. See I've learned that

over my life I may not have been blessed with

consistency in having someone to teach me how to become a man, but I was blessed with glimpses of how a man should carry himself. When I think about it, it's actually an awesome blessing to see it from so many different perspectives. It laid the blueprint for who I would become over the years. Yes, I failed at my marriage and, no I won't make excuses as to why I failed, but what I can give you is my takeaway. It has taken me a few years to realize that I even learned anything, but I have and part of the reason why I now can give you my story as well as my takeaway from the experience.

My father-in-law, for whom I still have the utmost respect, gratitude and admiration for until this very day, showed me that a man should always be able to humble himself when he has not stood firm to his word. You are not weak because you have apologized due to your misconduct or falling short of your word. Also, that pride is the cancer of the weak and effortless man. My takeaways in which I hope is helpful for someone who may be entertaining the idea of marriage:

1) Communication skills are a must.

2) Commonalities

3) Friendship

4) Respect of each other's strengths.

5) God has to be the cornerstone that you both look to in your time of weakness.

6) Know that as a man you have to be willing to grow in different areas to make sure your connection to your wife is strong.

7) Know that you will fight for her and your family without distraction.

8) No one comes before her but God.

You have to be willing to fight for your growth but also be willing to ask for help, accept the fact that you need it if that is the case. Marriage can be a very beautiful thing and I pray to have the opportunity to have a second chance at it and use the learning lessons I gained from my first marriage to fuel the success of a second marriage, if given the opportunity.

CHAPTER TWELVE: IF YOU THINK YOU'RE LONELY NOW…

I have had a lot of women in my life over the years. It's funny how as men we rarely discuss among ourselves about the times that we've actually have had our heart broken by a woman. I guess because it shows vulnerability and what effects it has on us. Well, I think about the few times I've experience this over my lifetime and how I have tried to block it from my memory.

I sometimes wonder why my success in relationships has not always been the best, and how I have struggled to be faithful, and again this is not to make excuses for my actions. It's truly an opportunity to have someone learn from my errors and challenges in my life. To be dreadfully honest, I feel like I've only been truly in love four times in my life. All four times it has not fully worked out for me for whatever the reason.

I sometimes think that my reckless disregard for a woman's feelings at times has bitten me in my butt a few times, however it never works out for me when I'm totally vulnerable with my feelings. I have learned that in this journey of love it's not always about the completed puzzle, but more about the task of putting the puzzle together.

There was this one female that had my heart and to this day still has somewhat of a special place in my heart, let's call her CRP for privacy purposes. This woman had my heart and you could not tell me that she wasn't the woman I was going to marry. Even to this day she and I can go years without speaking and she somehow always seems to find me. Because we have so much history, it's like no matter the situation or how long it's been she knows how to make my heart smile. A true lesson in manhood is acknowledging the power of a woman and the impact she can have on you when you truly decide to let go and open your heart. CRP to me is one of the most beautiful persons to ever enter my life as she and I could always laugh together and it felt so good, but somehow life just would not allow us to be in the same place and same time as we grew older.

I always thought CRP was that woman for me but it never happened, even though we tried. She left for the military, while I left for college. I remember she and I having a major falling out before I left for college and I figured I would never hear from her again, on top of that about a year later I got word that she had become pregnant. That news broke my heart, it felt like someone had kicked me in my chest then stabbed me in my heart when I received that news.

I think that was when I learned that love hurts. At nineteen years of age it really felt like I had a broken heart, but some would say it does not count because I was too young. I was sick for about three days but tried to mask it and submerge myself into talking to other women on my yard, and having as much sex as possible because in my mind that's how a man dealt with being hurt by a woman. Truly not dealing with it at all and showing no weakness was the best way to deal, I thought. My second semester sophomore year, I'm sitting in my dorm room around nine pm with my two crazy roommates from Philly, Henry Kyle Weaver and Mark Tyree Wilson. My phone rings as I go to answer it, the last person I was expecting to be on the other end was CRP. Now, when she and I had our last conversation it was the night before I left

for college in August of 1994 and she had none of

my contact information for me at school. My whole

freshman year I hadn't spoken to CRP, but this

night was about to change all that once my phone

rang in my dorm room. As I answer the phone she

says hello, and instantly I know it's her, my heart

drops and I looked as if I'd just seen a ghost. My

roommates were worried about me asking was I ok

and did something happen back home in Philly.

I'm like no everything is ok, but I never had

so many feelings and emotions rush through my

body at one time before in my life. We stayed on

the phone for a few hours. I found out she decided

to enroll in the military and had left college to go

into the Navy. You know I never fully understood

why she had the effect she had on me but that night

we made it all good and had agreed to attempt to try

to work on a relationship which did not work out at all in the long run.

I tell the story of CRP because I feel every man has had a CRP in his life. There was truly a breakdown in communication in which I think she and I missed each other in the midst of growing up and our paths flowing in entirely different directions. For whatever reason it just didn't work out and you could never understand why. The struggle is even harder when you've never had your heart broken and you don't know how to handle it nor were you ever instructed on what the impact may have on you.

Events like that were times I wish that I had the relationship with my father, or a father figure to pick up the phone and discuss the matter and get a little advice on how it should be handled. I truly believe because of our history it played a very huge part in our attachment.

I remember back in my high school days I was literally fighting few dudes from my neighborhood for an entire week. One night she called me because she had received word that I was fighting and this woman jumped on the bus and came to my house to make sure I was good. At that moment I knew there was something different about her. A woman like this is rare, like seeing a purple unicorn crossing the street, in my mind. I can recall us deciding to make an attempt to actually have a relationship even though we were not in the same state but I was so in love with this woman that I had to take a chance. This was my opening audition to understanding that love could hurt; this particular situation showed me.

What I do know is that it hurt, and bad. I remember that year 1994, coming home for Christmas break and K-Ci and JoJo, from the 90's group *Jodeci* had an album called *Love Always.* They had a remake on their album called *If You Think You're Lonely Now*, which was originally written by the late great Bobby Womack. This song killed me my entire time home. I was sick and couldn't wait to get back out of Philly since we were both from Philly and she wasn't in town with me. I couldn't wait to go back to school because I had never felt that type of hurt before, and being home wasn't helping in any way.

My aunt kept asking what was wrong and I couldn't explain it to her. I remember being up at 6:30 in the morning for my train back to North Carolina, which did not leave until noon that day, but I wanted out of Philly fast. The whole time I was home on break they kept playing the song on the radio. I felt like I was being punished by the hour. As I look back on the experience even up to this very day I think my loneliness played a part because I think she had a way of soothing me, so I became attached. Though she may have never been meant to be more than what she had become in my life, I think deep down inside she satisfied something for me that was fitting at that time and truthfully maybe that was her whole entire purpose, no more no less.

I have had two other times in my life where I have had my heart broken, what I learned is love comes with no instruction manual. We all choose how we deal with it but I can't act as if it hasn't had an impact on me. Sometimes I believe subconsciously it hinders me from being truly open to other women. I feel like some women say they want a particular type of man but when that man presents himself they're not ready, but I can say the same for us as men.

The conclusion I've come to is, what's for you is for you and a lot of times our experiences are our growth. It forces you to look outside of your normal, to expand one's mind, heart and attitude towards relationships.

I mention relationships because I believe as young boys there are habits and seeds planted in us that women are to be conquered. You don't have to show too much emotion, as this is a sign of weakness. We tend to move about as if women are situations of temporary pleasure and are replaceable. Sex is our biggest motive and how many women we can feast on, because this is a so-called sign of misguided manhood. In my mistakes in relationships I've always struggled with some level of loyalty in which is a part of the reason I haven't had many relationships. We place ourselves in plenty situations because we have this stupid fear we're going to miss out on something versus appreciating what we have in front of us: the woman who is interested in us.

In many ways, our growth is critical in truly becoming a man. The issue is we tend to fight growth when it comes to relationships; in the childish mindset of always thinking or feeling there is something better. The fear of becoming a man has levels in which we have to be willing to embrace and not hide behind our foolish immaturity. Granted I've learned that women are a species God has given us with no instructional manual, and we as men will never fully understand, but on the other end they are one of his true perfections.

I had an encounter or should I say a situation which caused me to step back and ask myself what was it that I really wanted. Let's call her Reds, this woman to me had the most beautiful spirit and you couldn't tell me that she wasn't something special. I mean I actually thought I heard God tell me she was the one. Yeah, I was tripping but everything about her was so calming to me and she had a way about her that fed my sapiosexuality. I was crazy about her way of thinking. I also loved her smell and her soft lips; I mean you couldn't tell me I hadn't run into my queen. I felt I was mature enough to handle this one and was willing to fight for what I thought would be 'us'. You can't change anyone who doesn't want to change, nor can you get someone to give you his or her heart that isn't offering it to you no matter how hard you try. A broken heart is a very emotional ride that as men we at times try to act as if we are not affected. There are some men who can become just as devastated as women, but this goes back to how I mentioned communication is critical; be aware of the signs. There were apparent signs that Reds was not that into me, but in my mind I thought that I could show her and it would change her feelings and mind.

There were apparent obstacles but when you have someone that's willing to ride with you those obstacles just become bumps in the road. Particularly when you have done all that you said you would do. It makes it that much harder because in your mind you're like why was I honest if this was going to be the result of my honesty. Reds had a way of making me melt in my thoughts about our possibility because despite our twists and turns. There is something about her that my heart was so glued to but I think it was more about her spirit that my heart was in tune with. When she and I would have conversation, I felt she had a way of speaking with my soul. In the end, it may all have just been in my mind wishing for something that may have never really been there from the start. I try to learn a lesson from every experience good or bad, and in my mind when things of this nature happen to me, when I'm super vulnerable it blows up in my face. I feel it's life's payback for me not being as in tune in other situations. This woman's beauty was so breathtaking that you can lose yourself in her eyes looking at the beauty of her soul. But I have also learned that in my struggles with relationships that sometimes not getting the person you think you want can be so much more of blessing than you will truly realize later in life. Love is a thing we all struggle, with both men and women. The difference is, we men are sometimes more boys than we are men when it comes to love and relationships. I have acquired the stigma of being somewhat of a ladies' man, but by no choice of my own. I would have to own up to it in many ways because I had to create the scenario to acquire that label. A part of my growth I have recognized is being able to accept my part in that of which I have created.

He who loses in love gains in experience to explore true joy in the opportunity to be with the right woman who fits the energy and love you seek. You will appreciate it so much more that you will take no day with this woman lightly; as you remind yourself of the journey that has gotten you to this very moment with this very special person you've so desired. I embark on this journey of an on-going evolving search for love, education, truth and humility. One thing for sure that I'm learning, is that manhood has nothing to do with having all the answers or aggressive attitude, nor is it defining oneself by society's definition. Manhood is the wiliness to learn from your mistakes, willingness to admit you're wrong, and being open to love hard while standing for something that has meaning and purpose to you as man.

CHAPTER THIRTEEN:
AMERIKKKA & BLACK MEN

Clearly from all the recent events we have had across America when it comes to the value of life, black men have been in question. One could say that life for a black man in America, has its challenges when it comes to our interactions with police and other black men; to say the least it hasn't been the best of situations. We have created an ongoing battle around what masculinity is and how we engage with one another. How is it that black men and our interaction with police can go so far left so easily? What's more important to me is, why is it our interactions with each other as black men can go so far left so easy so fast that it results into someone losing his life? I feel the fear of becoming a man is so far out of reach in the mind of our young people because they feel they have no reason

to live and have no expectations of living beyond

the age 18 to 21.

The lack of role models in the community

and the permeating sensationalizing of drama,

killing, and homosexuality, it is killing the very

fabric of our community. When you look at our

ever-shrinking Philadelphia educational system, the

removal of after school programs has a lot of these

young boys feeling helpless. Our community has

the highest incarceration of men, so a lot of women

are left to fend for themselves and our children. I

feel we also have to have the elder men of the

communities step up and assist the young men who

are trying to make a difference and stop living in

fear of these little boys who think they are men.

In my experience in working with a lot of

these young men they just want to feel like they are

loved, and can ask questions to get some answers. As I transition into my forties, I'm starting to see things a little differently; being out here in these streets trying to make a difference in my community I'm understanding the fight has to be a united front of real men willing to make a difference. Knowing that the growing pains for black boys are totally different than that of white boys we have to be willing to get dirty to save our kids.

The fight doesn't have to be as hard if we show them a different way but also afford them opportunities to be creative and expressive. We must remind them that we all make mistakes but we don't want to make mistakes that will impact the rest of your life in a negative way. We have to show parents that they have to stand up for their kids and stop allowing the school district to throw our kids away by limiting the resources that are provided to them. Again, I charge the men of our community to stand up and spearhead the charge to save our kids knowing that our women will support us as they have always done, but the change starts with us. We can't continue to holler we are men but not take charge, as we all know in the end a closed fist has a stronger impact than an open hand. This is why we have to become more united in our community and stop allowing or waiting on others to fix our own issues. We have to clean our own house because when we do this, we then afford ourselves the opportunity to slow or even stop the killings by cops but more importantly by other young black males.

Fear of becoming a man is real in our community so we have to stop allowing our boys to guess what a man should look and feel like; as well as stop allowing outside forces to create the image for them. There are currently 323 prisons in the state of Pennsylvania, five of them are right here in Philly, and our boys/men are the dominant population of those 323 prisons.

CHAPTER FOURTEEN: GOD'S GRACE

I take the impact and lack of care around our youth very personal because I know firsthand how easy it is to make bad choice that you may be unable to rebound from. When I was 26, I lived in the Washington, DC area. I had been residing there for about three years and was having some struggles. I had this friend at the time I knew from my college years that happened to be from Philly also. He had asked me if I could shoot up to Philly with him one day, I was unaware of the true nature of this trip but I found out once we arrived. We ended up on City Line Ave at the *Fridays* where his brother was awaiting our arrival. They discuss something and my man grabs a pound of marijuana from his brother and we jump back in the car and head back to Maryland where I lived, he went on to

Virginia where he lived. Now we just ignored the fact that we had now travelled between three to four states with drugs and had we been pulled over it, would have been major issues, but we didn't, so it didn't matter to us. The ironic part was I made no money off this transaction nor was I a weed head like he was, but he was my friend so I thought I was being a friend, STUPID on so many levels.

Well I decided, hell I have the same connections at home so why can't I shoot home and grab me some marijuana from my very close connection easily with no questions. Here's one of those moments in life where you think you're a man but you're really thinking and moving like a little boy who's easily influenced, and this little boy decision almost changed my entire life permanently. Well I did just that, jumped on 95 North and shot up to Philadelphia to talk to a family friend and convinced him to get me a pound of marijuana. He gave me a hard time, all he kept saying was *your sister will kill me if something happened to you over a pack.* Somehow, I convinced him and he gave in and gave it to me. I was excited and thought I was about to make a big man's move, as I totally disregarded my safety and the fact that I was now carrying illegal drugs across state lines; disregarding the trouble I would get into had I been pulled over by the Delaware or Maryland police.

Well I made it back to Maryland. I lived with my best friend, and his girlfriend at the time lived with us as well. We had moved into the Silver Spring area of Maryland from Northwest Washington, DC. On this particular night, my best friend was out on the town with his girlfriend. I had my man from Philly over to show him the pound of weed I had and needed his assistance bagging it up.

Little did I know this was going to be a life changing night. I was not prepared for all that would happen. So, we have the weed spread across the dining room table with the music playing, talking, laughing and breaking up the weed to bag up. There was a new NAS album out and I had it in my car, he wanted to hear it so he asked where it was. I'm like *man it's outside in the car here's my keys go grab it out of the CD player.* He goes out to the car. I'm unaware that my neighbor had called the police about my music that wasn't even being played loudly. I hear this knock at the door, and the first thing I think is my dude had now locked himself out.

I go to the door talking shit like *dude how the hell did you lock yourself out?* Remember we have all the marijuana laid across the table but I open the door thinking it's going to be him, but hell naw it's a cop. I freeze up not sure why he's here or what I should do next as I have this white cop standing at my door with his hand on his gun. First thing he says "*I smell something, are you smoking any illegal drugs in here?*"

My heart is now racing hard and about to jump clear out of my chest, but I have to play it cool. I was actually becoming stupid by the second as I totally forgot in that split moment that we had a pound of weed laid across my table. While in my stupidity, I say to the officer. no and swing my door open and invited him in. He steps in and walks back to my best friend's room and walks right past the table. I noticed it and I try to move it but he comes running back out the room with his gun cocked and pointed at me. Here is that moment you realize you have just truly FUCKED up and threw all common sense out of the window. In my mind I'm thinking *how stupid are you dude to invite this cop into your home without a search warrant?* Next thing I know I have about ten cops in my apartment with dogs and all.

I've now been handcuffed to the chair and being grilled with questions. To make matters worse, my best friend walks in and they start asking him questions. My man that went to the car never came back in at all. I was out there on an island all by myself trying to be a so-called man in my mind. It was time to pay the piper as I just threw my career away at *Enterprise Rent-A-Car*, and almost had my best friend caught up in some bullshit as this is the reckless mistakes we make trying to be something we're not. The cop takes me out handcuffed and all and puts me in the front seat, which was shocking, and on to Rockville, Maryland police station to book me with a drug charge.

First getting locked up is crazy on so many levels. You're violated as soon as you start the process of being booked. I mean you're damn near stripped naked and asked to bend over for a cavity search. I have never felt so violated in my life. My mind was racing 100 miles a minute trying to figure out what have I just done to totally screw up my life. They take my fingerprints; ask me all types of questions, then throw me in a holding cell where I sat for about five hours. What blew my mind was sitting in this cell with about seven strangers and all seven of these dudes seemed way too comfortable, as a few of them were asleep as if they were home in their own bed. Okay, now I'm numb to the situation as I kept asking myself why did I put myself in this situation and what's about to happen to me?

As I'm sitting in this little ass cell, all I kept saying was *how could you disappoint Aunt Rochelle, grandma and your sister?* Even though they were all unaware of what was going on I felt like a disappointment. I'm sitting there not knowing what was going to happen next. This one dude kept saying if we were in there six hours we were going to get fitted for our orange jump suit and sent over to the prison. I'm scared and mad because this dude won't shut up and these other dudes are snoring like they're at home. What the hell did I get myself into? It's almost the sixth hour and the next thing I know I hear my name called, *"Richard Sutton."* *"Yes, Officer!"* He said, *"We are letting you go on your own recognizance."* I had no idea what recognizance meant at the time but I understood 'let go' and man was I happy.

The journey this would take me on started as soon as I was released that night as it was about 2:30 in the morning and I had no money or no cell phone so I couldn't call anyone to come get me. I had to walk about three miles and as I walked this long road at the end was a strip mall, there's a cab sitting there as if it were waiting on me. Let's sidebar for a moment: I believe faith is a very real thing and sometimes we are put in situations by self-inflection or just life's struggles and our faith is challenged. This situation I was experiencing was a true walk and test of my faith. Believing everything my grandmother who happened to be a pastor would talk about with my cousins and I growing up, all the time. Now mind you, I never called home and informed my family what I was going through, nor did I want them worrying about me calling everyday making the situation more challenging for me. Plus, this was a decision I made, so I had to fall on my sword.

When I came across this cab sitting in the shopping mall parking lot at two something in the morning I was happy, and I was tired from sitting so long then having to walk three miles. I swear to you I jumped in this cab and went right to sleep. I don't recall giving the driver my information or anything, but I had to as the next thing I know this older Caucasian gentleman who could have been in his mid-fifties or early sixties said, "*young man wake up, you're home.*" He had a very calming demeanor about him that was very soothing. I recall waking up discombobulated, I said thank you, stepped out the car as he asked was I ok. He pulled off without charging me. I walked into the house exhausted so I went right to bed scared and not sure of my future because I made a very stupid move and was about to pay the consequences for my actions. I had to find a lawyer plus the cop that was completing my paperwork said it was very important that I find a lawyer.

The next day I started my quest to find an attorney and I found one but this guy was unique because out of all the lawyers I could have picked in the DC Metropolitan area I find a lawyer from my hometown of Philadelphia, who grew up not too far from me in Chestnut Hill. My first visit to him we talked about home for about 15 minutes, which was funny because in my mind I kept thinking this little white guy knows nothing about my area of town when in fact he did, we connected. He decided to charge me half price because we both were from home. We reviewed my case he said *"Are you aware they're trying to charge you with a drug kingpin charge which is a minimum of 15 and a max of 30 years?"* I swear my heart fell out of my chest. For a pound of weed they were trying to send me to prison that long for something that small? The harsh reality had kicked me in my gut and I felt like I wanted to throw up my breakfast and anything else in his office. My world was upside down and now I'm really scared but can't call home. Getting caught up in the justice system is the worst feeling ever but when you're young and thoughtless you feel invincible, but this day I felt like my soul was snatched out of my body. As I left his office that day all I could do was think about how the American justice system and black men were like oil and water. I felt so sick that day that I attempted to get something to eat on my way home but felt nauseous so I was unable to eat. I went home, got in bed and slept for an entire day. I attempted to slow my thoughts down but was unsuccessful.

They say prayer changes things and they say faith is something you must trust and we usually don't think to pray consistently when running the streets until something major happens. I'm embarrassed to say it but I was one of those very people but I honestly believe that when you have people praying for you even when you're not praying, God allows angels to cover you even in your stupidity. The old folks like to say God protects babies and fools. I was one of the biggest fools there was, because I knew better from just family history alone that this was something I should have kept my ass far away from, but as my mother would say *"A hard head makes a soft ass every time."* I had to wait a little over thirty days for my court date. Let me tell you, those thirty plus days felt like five damn years, as I was unaware of what my fate may be. In my mind I couldn't stop thinking about those possible thirty years that was hanging over my head; it was driving me crazy.

My court date comes in mid-October, and I swear every day it came closer to the date, I felt like someone was punching me in the back of my head as I had continuous migraines. I kept telling myself that I couldn't break because this is all due to a decision I decided to make; I had to man up. Please don't get me misunderstood because this was not a stance of bravery or bravado of any sort, but an effort to stand as a man since I decided to make the moves that put me in this situation. I met with my lawyer for a quick briefing prior to our start time for court so we could discuss what was about to happen and how he felt things might play out. Here is the sad truth: I heard nothing he was saying because my mind was programming for the worst. I understood my position and who put me here but I also couldn't stop thinking of how unsuccessful I know black men are in court versus white males when it comes to the same crimes.

As we walked into the courtroom, a calm came over me that I can't really explain; but I felt as if something or someone walked into the courtroom with me that day.

I remember the judge coming to the bench. He was a slim built white guy with a clean cut and military style haircut. As he and my attorney went back and forth, as there was no jury present, I remember my attorney saying *"this young man has no priors your honor and he's a hardworking man that works for Enterprise Rent-A-Car and college educated. He made a very bad judgment call in this one your honor."* The judge said a few things back to him as he questioned my character and my choices, but remember I said I felt like I walked into court with someone else, a higher power. Well the next thing I know I hear my attorney say *"can we agree upon two years' probation, and if he completes his probation without any slip ups, then can we also agree to have all charges expunged from his record?"* The judge sat back in his seat looked at me and said *"any slip ups I will charge him with the entire full count."* My heart was rejoicing with so much joy that I could hardly contain myself. No time served, probation, and expungement; how I knew this was nothing but GOD is because there is no way you can explain to me how from the very start of this whole situation things were happening that were unexplainable to me. I truly believe in my heart of hearts that I was given a second chance to help save another young life that may feel as I felt prior to that court case. I mean I almost threw my entire life away for one very bad judgment call. As a 24-year-old black male walking away from the US judicial system was a feat in and of itself. This is a large factor as to why I feel I owe it to my community and myself to save as many young black and brown males as possible, and help them to avoid the pitfalls of my mistakes in the same type of situation. They may not come out unscathed as I did.

In 2016, I created The Amari Academy to help young males between the ages of 12 to 18. The Amari Academy has a focus on leadership; self-respect; money mindset; how to treat and speak to a woman; and self-expression through journal writing. These are the key attributes I find I struggled with in my younger years because had I truly respected myself, I would not have made the bad choice of attempting to sell drugs for truly no apparent reason. Just another twist and turn of becoming man, acknowledging that I was making immature decisions with reckless regard and those who loved me as well as myself.

There is a scripture that I think sums up my life and the lesson from this process. That scripture is Jeremiah 29:11 it reads, *"For I know the plans I have for you."* Declares the Lord, He plans to prosper you and not harm you, plans to give you hope and a future.

The fear of becoming a man can sometimes be forced upon you in a manner that you're just not ready to face but have no choice. There comes a time when you have to put your personal feelings on the back burner and find a way to stand as best as possible for yourself.

CHAPTER FIFTEEN: MY YOUNG PRINCE

One of my biggest struggles in my life and true heartbreak like no other, in which the hurt is still very present to this day, is the hurt I have for the dismantled relationship I have with my 15-year-old son. The pain I bear on a daily basis is unexplainable as this is a hurt I don't truly care to speak of often. Someone always tries to tell you what you should do or should be doing in your situation even though they've never spent a day in your shoes. First allow me to state that this is not an attempt to attack any one particular individual in an effort to make myself look better in any way. I never wanted kids outside of wedlock because I wanted to be different, but hadn't truly accepted manhood… well at least I thought I did, but hindsight is 20/20.

The hurt is unbelievable when your child is completely turned against you. This is not because you don't care about them or support them, nor is it a situation where you attempted to run from your responsibility as a father. Nope, that's far from the case but all the very opposite; I have a true emptiness in my heart that can't be fixed, and the family court system in my opinion is the worst when it comes to fathers and our fight for our kids. Every experience I've had with the family court system over the past 14 years has been a horrible experiences on every account. Ladies, I know it easy to say that black men are deadbeats and we don't want to take care of our kids, and that may be a true statement in some cases, but it's not across the board. Using our kids as get back, in the end, does more damage to the kid than it does to the father. My father wasn't the best of fathers nor was he the worst. What I can say is, I never remember my mother attempting to turn me against him or bad mouthing him to me. I never heard her say a bad word about him my entire life.

I have endured so much pain over the years due to the lack of communication and heartache that I have had with my son's mother. I would be the first to admit that this was not the ideal situation to bring a child into as she and I were never a couple nor was there an effort to become one, but I have made countless attempts to resolve whatever issues that would hinder the efforts of co-parenting our son, but every effort I've made has been met with anger and deceitfulness. I pray everyday that some sort of change comes so that I can have an opportunity to be father to my son. I'm out here making an effort to help and expose other young black males to ride the correct side of the tracks and avoid the traps, but can't even do it for my own flesh and blood.

The last time I attempted to go to family court, I sat in this white woman's office as she attempted to speak at me and not to me. She was so disrespectful as she treated me like I was a criminal; I mean these people are so damn rude and disrespectful that you have to pray to keep from totally snapping out. This lady attempted to berate me and minimize my efforts and state incorrect facts and as I would attempt to correct her errors, she would just become more disrespectful. As this woman would talk to me as if I was a piece of shit, she states that I was required by court order to pay health insurance for my son. I stated to her that she was incorrect but I do currently pay for his health insurance and child support as well. She yelled at me and says, "*so what you should want to do it anyway, court order or not.*" I said, "*why are you speaking to me in this manner? This is truly unacceptable.* She screams at the top of her lungs, "*SECURITY come remove this man from my office immediately.*" Now I'm stuck, because it's my word against hers so, I walk out of her office and followed security to the elevator. Here's how the rest of my ride went with Philadelphia family court professionals as I use that word very lightly. I asked to speak to this lady's supervisor; they made me wait for 15 minutes. Then next thing I know this very large white woman gets off the elevator with an attitude and proceeds to ask can she help me. I start to explain myself, she rudely cuts me off while never formally introducing herself nor does she give me her full name.

I'm upset but I love my son and I can't afford to allow this woman to pull me off my square. When I know she'll play victim and have me locked up so I decided to walk away and lick my wounds on my way back to my car. I decided to call back and speak to the real supervisor because I have the original woman's name whose office I sat in. I call and I'm put on hold for 15 minutes and someone finally comes back to the phone. I explain my situation and how they have given this woman's name that's supposed to be the supervisor of that particular department. Ok now I'm getting somewhere well, at least that's what I thought was about to happen, but hell no. This was the most horrible experience as I was passed around for about 45 minutes until I got this gentleman on the phone. I tell him the situation and the name of this lady I was given as the manager of this department so lets say her name was Ms. Baxter. I give her name and he asked me to repeat the name three times, now I'm getting more frustrated. The next thing I know he says *"sir where did you get Ms. Baxter's information?"* I said *"the same department of the woman who was speaking to me as if I was a child."* He says, *"sir, Ms. Baxter has been deceased for three years."* In that exact moment I gasp for air as I felt like I was just punched in the gut. I cannot explain to you the anger and rage that passed through my body. I now had total loss of respect for the family court system as a whole at that very moment. I spent an entire day dealing with this issue to have been given the run around by these low class people was unbelievable.

My journey with my son has been one of disappointment and heartache on so many levels. I have made countless efforts to engage my son to become the father I truly never had. So, the

countless nights of having a broken heart because

his mother feels that I'm not worthy of parenting

my son for whatever reason, hurts. I will never

understand why women feel using the child to hurt

the father is the best move, because in the end the

child is paying the price more than anyone. I have

dealt with pain in my life, as I'm sure we all have

but to be brutally honest there is no pain like having

someone turn your child against you. I actually

have my son's name tattooed on the inside of my

right forearm. It was a summer day, and I was

supposed to get my son this day, I was excited to

see him. Well just like clockwork his mother

decided that I shouldn't see him. She was now upset

with me over something I can't recall the particular

issue. I was so hurt that I went out with my friend

Joi because she wanted me to get the situation off

my mind. We ended up on South Street, and she says to me *"are you serious about getting that tattoo we discussed in the car?"* I said, *"yes, why not? I needed to get my emotions in check today"* as we walked into this tattoo shop to look at their work.

We honed in on this one tattoo artist as we watched him work on another person and he impressed me. I looked through a few designs in the book that was displayed on a glass table. But I changed my mind and decided to have him freehand my son's name on the inside of my forearm. As I mentioned, this was a very rough day due to my son's mother denying me access to see him. I was beyond hurt, but getting this tattoo that day really made me feel a lot better because in my mind I felt like he was now with me daily.

This is among countless situations where I've had issues with his mother for whatever reason she felt on whatever particular day. One of the things that bothers me the most about our frequent drama was my son has always played the pawn. I went through a period of true hate for my son's mother that embodied everything unhealthy about our lack of co-parenting for my son. Allow me to step back and give a little history on the two of us.

My son's mother and I attended the same high school, as she was in a different building participating in an accelerated program. We interacted a few times briefly during our freshman and junior year very, very briefly. If you would have told me back in high school that she and I would have a child together, I would have laughed at you so hard, in disbelief. Well, we completed high school and I go off to college and she goes on with her life. I didn't think I would ever run into her and especially not in a capacity in which we would start messing around. Hell, I returned from college in 1998 faced with the fact that I had dropped out of college and returned to Philadelphia. I had aspirations of becoming an actor and doing some modeling. Clearly that didn't work out for me so now I was on a mission to find myself as I was just wandering through life at the tender age of 22 years old.

Having a really hard time, I had decided I wanted to move to Washington, DC but wasn't sure how I was going to accomplish this move. At this time, I was doing a lot of partying with friends and running the street. I remember attending an event at this bar called *Champagnes* in the Germantown area of Philly. I was partying hard this night drinking and laughing all night and I remembering going upstairs to see what was going on and see her sitting there. We made eye contact so I decided to walk over to her and we embraced and started to catch up on life since we hadn't seen each other since high school. We talked for a few and she gave me her number to give her a call sometime. I remember holding on to the number for about two or three weeks before calling. The crazy part was I wasn't going call and I have had days where I wish I had not made that call, I swear. I wouldn't have this big-eyed kid that looks exactly like me running around in this world—without me. There has to be no greater blessing in the world than to be blessed with a healthy child and a boy to keep your bloodline strong and relevant.

I understand despite the challenges that have been set in motion, I will always move to create a better life for him and his future so, he will have opportunities that were not afforded to me. I could

never truly explain to him why his mother feels the

way she does. Why she feels that everyone else

around her is a better fit to teach him about life and

growing up as a young black male in America. It's

true pain at the highest point. Allow me to give you

an example of the pain I have endured for the last

15 years, but better yet most recent. My son's

mother decided that I shouldn't see our child

because I checked him after being on the phone

with him. He was disrespectful towards me. I

checked him and we hang up. Five minutes later, as

expected, his mother calls me screaming and

hollering asking who do I think I am?

This is the type of dysfunction that would be

constant in the attempt to build a father son

relationship with my son. Once again, he's kept

from me and fed some negativity about me and at

this point he is supposed to be afraid of me. Fast forward my son is now fifteen years of age and sees me standing outside a friend's business. At the same time, I feel his presence but unsure because he's walking and looking away from me so that I would be unable to see his face. I can't stop staring at this 5'10" boy walking past me, and as I'm looking him up and down, my spirit is telling me it's him. As he gets in front of me, he starts to walk abruptly at a faster pace while looking to the other side of the street. I feel it's him but wasn't sure and didn't want to chase down someone else's kid if I was wrong.

The pain of knowing your child has a fear or issue with you when you've never done anything to them to warrant this emotion is brutal to say the least. Later that night I received a phone call from my son's grandmother and she says, *"Rich were you on the avenue today?"*

"Yes! Ma'am I was on the avenue today."

She says, *"You don't know your son when you see him?"*

Apparently, my son was aware that I was standing there and he decided he didn't want to talk to me nor see me. He also felt the need to inform his mother that he had seen me. Well, as soon as his grandmother finished her statement I knew exactly what she was talking about. I start describing what he had on and she said, *"I'm not sure what he had on, I didn't see him today. I just received a call from his mother and he told her he had seen you. I'm actually happy you weren't sure it was him; because he said had you noticed him he was going to run from you."*

"Why would he run from me?" I asked.

She informs me, *"He said he's scared of you from when you scolded him that night on the phone."*

It felt like someone had stuck a dagger in my heart and rib all at the same time, as I broke down in tears on the phone with his grandmother. I do not believe there are any perfect parents walking this Earth, and with that said I blame myself for the pain I have caused my son and myself. Everyone is quick to say run to the courts but over the years I have been to court on countless times with no success. My biggest frustration has always been that I've never denied my son nor have I ever made myself inaccessible to him. I always wanted to be more for my son than my father was for me, but the difference here is that my mother never at any point attempted to bad mouth my father to me, nor did she try to make anyone else out to be more of father or man to me growing up. My frustration and attempts to make peace with his mother has always fallen on deaf ears. Anytime I had my son I would always reassure him that I loved him and told him that he could be or do anything he wanted in this world. I struggle because I have created an academy for youth my son's age and it kills me because I'm not teaching my own son these skills and he's scared of me.

The feeling of hurt is so infinite. How does one hate the person that they've conceived a child with, and this person despite the situation has never abandoned you? I pray that at some point sooner than later she sees that our relationship as parents is so much bigger than the two of us and this is a lifetime commitment that we both have to share.

To my son if you ever have the opportunity to read these words it's not to minimize your mother or to make myself look as if I've

been faultless in your life. What I want you

to know is there is no love like the love a

father could have for his son. As I write

these words, I pray that one day you and I

can sit and discuss all your inquisitive

questions of a young boy wondering why his

father wasn't always present.   Know that

there has never been a day that I attempted

to turn my back on you. Someday you may

have a son of your own and I want to be

able to navigate you through the challenges

and pitfalls that I could have avoided. My

job in this world is to give you the proper

tools for manhood and wise counsel when

needed. Even though my father was not as

active in my life, I live by a biblical scripture

that was taught to me by my grandmother at

a very young age. It reads, "Honor thy mother and thy father that your days will be long upon the Earth". Despite the flaws and mistakes of your mother and me you should understand that there is no perfect parent, our mistakes are those that will be an inner struggle for the both of us, especially for me until the day of my death. My mindset around how I feel about the battle and challenges of my effort to just be an active present father in your life has been very hard. I have so many emotions, with countless nights of crying and writing in my journal as to why this has been such a difficult journey to just be a loving father. I pray none of the situations you've witnessed nor the seeds of dislike planted in your mind for me have a negative impact on your life long term. Also, know that as your father, I will always be a resource for you to come to for guidance, love, understanding and support. You are a young king who has no limitations in life but the ones you allow others or your own mind to set for you. I need you to understand that this world is truly about perspective and looking at the glass half full and also understand you will have challenges that your white counterparts will never attempt to understand, You sir, walk in greatness with no limitations on your possibilities in this world. You sir, are loved by many and you have family on both sides supporting your future success and as your father I'm appointed with laying the road map for you to avoid my missteps and bad decisions to the best of my ability. Please, understand

your mother and I are both flawed but filled

with love when it comes to you. Become who

you're destined to become, shoot for Mars

so if you miss you'll still be among the stars

son. I'll love you until my last breath son

and with every breath I'm blessed with I

look to create a legacy to leave you. Move

through this thing called life with an

objective to always see yourself succeed in

whatever you put your mind too. A son is

God's way of blessing a man with a better

version then himself.

Son, this thing called life comes with no

instructions but your father has gained some

wisdom, which is the achievement of the

ability to give guidance. Son, your black

skin will cause your journey to achieve some of your goals in life a little harder than that of your counterpart. Meaning that your efforts, movement and process will have to be well thought out. There will be situations and people that will remind you that you are a black male. Here's what I want you to always remember. Listen to the music of your heart's desires son and allow no one to tell you that the life you look to create is not possible. Do not allow the faults of others to discourage your dreams but know as a black male your strength is your power to not fear failure. Tackle every challenge as if it's your last. Be creative, strong, and resilient, King status, document your goals and have consistent open dialogue with the Almighty man above.

Fear of becoming a man is truly about not holding onto the fear of the inevitable. Understanding that despite your circumstance of having an absentee father or present dad who has no idea of what a father looks like, you are blessed with opportunities to see real men in action and model those attributes of manhood in your life. Never be scared to ask for help or mentorship by those men you see handling themselves in a manor that's respectful and engaged. Remember manhood is an ever-ongoing process to the day you meet your maker and no one person has the absolute answer to the perfection of manhood and that's because there is none.

The only fear you should have is the fear of not becoming the man you are supposed to become. Fear not being a God-fearing man and/or fear the mediocrity not making the effort to create the life you dream of having. Fear looking yourself in the mirror and being disappointed with the man you see.

CHAPTER SIXTEEN: CHANGE FACTORS

I have traveled this life in a manner of some self-doubt due to my past struggles. I have allowed my thoughts of negative intentions to hinder the growth of the man God has set for me to become. I want my transparency to assist you the reader to move beyond your fears, self-doubt and internal whispers of failure to prosecute your higher level of greatness. What I mean is don't allow people or bad experiences to stop your growth as a man. The road map to greatness detours through the back streets of failure, which are unavoidable by all. But failure builds character as it forces you to stand in the battlement of truth or fall on the sharp sword of self-pity.

Do not fear becoming a man, but do fear allowing life to stagnate your truth and growth as a man. Be honest with yourself, while accepting your faults and imperfections in your constant growth to always become a better you. Are you willing to develop your mind in ways that you may not be used to doing, like reading? According to a Huffington Post article dated April 4, 2014 titled *"Black Children Face the Most Barriers to Success in America, Asians the least"* written by Rebecca Kline, states, *"Only 66% of African Americans graduate from high school on time."* These are very staggering and disappointing numbers for our community. More of the reason I stress, that as men, we have to be a very present structure in our communities. Think about that!

Although, I've had my family struggles and very strong insecurities that I would fight with daily; one undeniable fact I had in my family was love, and yes, at times I struggled with the acceptance of that love due to my insecurities. I recognize now that at no point did my family allow me to fall victim to the system or should I say in the arms of foster care. I truly believe we do at times take for granted those things in life that we think are just supposed to happen. The honest truth is, at any point my grandmother and both of my aunts could have turned their backs on me and said I was too much of an additional responsibility for them to carry.

Think about it, I added additional cost to their already financially strapped household. This is something I could truly never pay them all back for, but will always have a level of gratitude and thankfulness, for never giving up on me. I remember when I first went to my Aunt Rochelle's house she had no heat at the time and was using kerosene heaters to warm her home. Yet, she still opened her doors to me and allowed me to be apart

of her home. Yes, for a few weeks we had to warm

the water up on the stove in a pot and carry it up the

stairs and dump it in the tub to take a bath. I have

to be humbled by the strength of the women in my

family and I admire all they poured in to me

growing up as a boy. I always hear folks say, a

woman can't teach a boy to be a man and yes, I

agree somewhat, but I would have to say there is an

essence of truth and understanding that only a

woman could give a young boy about life and

becoming a man.

What happens is, a lot of times when we as

little boys become men, we look for the attributes

and traits displayed by our mothers in that of the

woman we take interest in. I think sometimes that's

part of the reason I struggle with being satisfied

with myself when it comes to women. I mean look,

I had four very awesome women that had a very big impact on my life. My mother is this loving overprotective woman that is a neat freak. Everything with her has to be extra clean no dirt whatsoever. My grandmother was this spiritual, loving woman that could be a real firecracker when she wanted too. My sister is this outgoing, very analytical, free-spirited ball of energy. My aunt tries to help everyone and be a support system to the entire family, and she is also a lot like my grandmother. It doesn't help that the older she gets, the more she looks like my grandmother.

I have become the man I am from my experiences in life as well as my continuous fight with my insecurities and self-doubt battles I've had over the years. The core of who I have become I must contribute to these wonderful women and all they have done for me, and the unconditional love that they have provided for me.

Webster's definition of fear says, "Fear, mean painful emotion of danger. Fear is the most general word and suggests great worry and usually loss of courage < fear of the unknown>."

We must not allow fear to cripple an entire generation of boys who may feel that they have no opportunity to win in this game called life. Even more importantly we have to teach the self-preservation and the importance of education and its benefits and how it will afford them the opportunity create options for themselves. It's apparent that there is a generation of young black women who are currently the most educated individuals in the country, so how do we raise the bar of our young men and show them the benefits and what it could create for our communities? Yes, our discussion has been the fear of becoming a man but we now have to kill the fear and create young kings who are willing to step up and be leaders, while not fearing the truth of being smart.

Having so many educated young women could truly change the dynamics as we encourage the young men to meet them at that higher educational level. The truth is that despite the ill disregard for the life of black males in this country, I do believe the empowerment of affordable education could be the change factor on both sides of the coin for us as black men. Meaning that the senseless so called black-on-black crime could be minimized drastically. Please note, I truly don't believe in so called black-on-black crime because crime is crime. There is no other nationality of people classified as cultural-on-cultural crime. I've never witnessed on the news them describing two white men partaking in a crime and one kills the other as white-on-white crime. We have to be aware of the cultural impact statements like black-on-black crime has on the psyche of a people.

Let's not mistake my comments as if there are no men in our communities stepping up, because there are plenty but the issue is there aren't enough of us moving as a unit to figure out how we could be more impactful in what it is we are trying to achieve. Let's take for example my home town of Philly, there is a lot of us making the effort to make a difference, but the issue in my opinion is a lot of us are moving as individuals instead of finding someone else with a like-minded agenda and partnering with them so we can move like a wolf-pack versus a lone wolf. I speak to this because I'm also at fault for this same action.

We have to become the change factor that dismantles the fear of becoming a man in our community and create the image for our boys to see what it means. But more importantly, it's vital for the core of our existence in protecting our women, children as well as our neighborhoods.

My awesome grandmother passed away a few years ago and as I remember sitting with her at her bedside, I asked her did she remember beating me as a kid with a switch off the tree? She beat me so bad that I had a mark on me until I was 19 years of age. Her response is one that will stick with me until God decides to take my last breath. She said, *"no baby I don't recall it, but let me ask you this, would you be the man you are had I not?"* As usual she leaves me speechless. Now how do you respond to a statement like that?

"Education is the passport to the future, for tomorrow belongs to those who prepare for it today."

~Malcolm X

Made in the USA
Lexington, KY
18 June 2018